# REAL WRITING

## FROM STRUCTURED PARAGRAPH TO COMPLETE ESSAY

Mariko Kawasaki
Ayed Hasian
Samuel Haugh
Yoko Nakano
Seishirou Ibaraki

Nan'un-do

# Real Writing
## From structured paragraph to complete essay

*Copyright © 2019*

Mariko Kawasaki
Ayed Hasian
Samuel Haugh
Yoko Nakano
Seishirou Ibaraki

*All rights Reserved.*

*No part of this book may be reproduced in any form without written permission from the authors and Nan'un-do Co., Ltd.*

このテキストの音声を無料で視聴（ストリーミング）・ダウンロードできます。自習用音声としてご活用ください。
以下のサイトにアクセスしてテキスト番号で検索してください。

**https://nanun-do.com**　テキスト番号 [ 511984 ]

※ 無線 LAN（WiFi）に接続してのご利用を推奨いたします。

※ 音声ダウンロードは Zip ファイルでの提供になります。
お使いの機器によっては別途ソフトウェア（アプリケーション）の導入が必要となります。

※ Real Writing 音声ダウンロードページは以下の
QR コードからもご利用になれます。

# HOW TO USE THIS TEXTBOOK

REAL ENGLISH is for beginners who are ready to learn how to write academic paragraphs and essays. When writing English compositions, you have to do more than just translate your Japanese writing. You have to organize your ideas logically and use vocabulary and grammar that are more formal than daily English conversation. It might sound difficult, but do not worry. REAL ENGLISH will make English writing easy for you. Every unit has sample paragraphs to show you proper structure as well as teach you words and grammar points that you can use. In addition, each unit is full of exercises you can use to practice with your classmates or by yourself. You are going to learn to write longer, more detailed paragraphs and essays of various kinds, but this book will guide you with samples, outlines, and templates that will help you every step of the way.

Although the first writing assignments will be simple five-sentence paragraphs, you will be challenged to write increasingly complex and detailed paragraphs as your skills grow with each chapter. Chapters 1-11 will focus on various paragraph styles that are important in academic writing. Next, you will learn how to summarize ideas in chapter 12. All of the writing skills you learn in these chapters will help you prepare for your final challenge, writing full essays of four or five paragraphs, which you will practice in chapters 13-15.

Each chapter is divided into different learning goals so that you can master detailed aspects of English writing. Part 1 gives models that demonstrate the writing goals for the unit as well as the logical flow of ideas that you should follow in your paragraphs. Part 2 breaks down the structure of the model paragraphs in easy-to-understand detail. In Part 3, you can practice using various writing tools to help you express your ideas. Finally, in Part 4, you will have the chance to combine everything you have learned in your own writing. You will use your new skills to complete partial paragraphs first and then gradually transition to writing full compositions of your own.

Remember that English writing is your chance to express yourself. By using REAL ENGLISH, you will be able to share your ideas by writing logical paragraphs that are detailed, accurate, and easy to understand. Soon, you will become a real English writer, too. Good luck!

We are grateful to the following teachers of School of Human Welfare Studies, Kwansei Gakuin University for their contribution:

- ★ Chapter 10 "The Wooden Bowl" LEE, Sunhye
- ★ Chapter 13 "The Power of Sports" HAYASHI, Naoya
- ★ Chapter 14 "Cultural Differences and Coaching Style" SASABA, Ikuko
- ★ Chapter 15 "Mindfulness, Why Not?" IKENO, Satoshi

HASIAN, Ayed
KAWASAKI, Mariko

# 本書の使い方

　初めて英語でひとまとまりの文章を書く人たちのために本書を作りました。ひとまとまりの文章を書く作業は、単なる和文英訳ではありません。内容を整理整頓して読み手にわかりやすく書くことや、会話とは異なる適切な形式に沿った表現を使うことなど、様々な点に留意が必要です。このような書くときの規則や、良い文章を書く技術を、モデル文章から学習してください。そのためにモデル文章はできるだけ平易にし、難しい単語には注釈をつけました。ペアやグループで、意見を交換しながら、どのような点を模倣するべきかを発見してください。そして最初はモデル文章をテンプレートにして自分の文章を書いてみましょう。

　第1章から第11章まではいろいろな種類の段落の書き方を学びます。第12章はすでにある文章を要約して1段落に表す方法を学びます。最後の第13章から第15章の3つの章は4、5段落からなるエッセイの書き方を学びます。エッセイ中のそれぞれの段落はここまで学んできた段落の基本と同じです。こんなに長い作文はたいへんと思わず、ぜひ大作にチャレンジしてみてください。

　各章では、まず学習目標を確認しましょう。Part 1 の Model を観察し、話の流れとその書き方の特徴を見つけましょう。Part 2 Structure では具体的に段落の構成を学びます。ここでも Model をしっかり観察・分析しましょう。Part 3 Writing Tools では書くときの約束（句読点や大文字の使い方）について学びます。最後に Part 4 Writing では自分で書いてみます。最初は段落の一部分だけを書くだけですが、だんだんと書く量を増やして、最終的に段落全体を書けるようにします。何を書くのか考えたり、整理したりする手法も紹介しています。

　さあ、書きたいことを書いてみましょう。書くときには決まりがあることを忘れないで、わからなくなったら本書を見直したり、調べたりしてください。きっと良い文章が書けます。

川﨑眞理子<br>
ハセイン・アイエド

---

本書の作成にあたり、関西学院大学人間福祉学部の先生方にご協力をいただきました。感謝申し上げます。

- ★ Chapter 10 "The Wooden Bowl" 李 善惠（LEE, Sunhye）
- ★ Chapter 13 "The Power of Sports" 林 直也
- ★ Chapter 14 "Cultural Differences and Coaching Style" 笹場 育子
- ★ Chapter 15 "Mindfulness, Why Not?" 池埜 聡

# CONTENTS

| | | | |
|---|---|---|---|
| Chapter | 1 | Explanatory Paragraphs | 06 |
| Chapter | 2 | Information Paragraphs | 12 |
| Chapter | 3 | Opinion Paragraphs | 18 |
| Chapter | 4 | Descriptive Paragraphs | 24 |
| Chapter | 5 | Comparative Paragraphs | 32 |
| Chapter | 6 | Contrast Paragraphs | 40 |
| Chapter | 7 | Cause and Effect Paragraphs | 48 |
| Chapter | 8 | Argumentative Paragraphs | 56 |
| Chapter | 9 | Problem and Solution Paragraphs | 64 |
| Chapter | 10 | Time-order Paragraphs | 72 |
| Chapter | 11 | Process Paragraphs | 80 |
| Chapter | 12 | Summaries | 88 |
| Chapter | 13 | Five Paragraph Essays | 96 |
| Chapter | 14 | Concluding Paragraphs for Essays | 104 |
| Chapter | 15 | Effective Ways to Begin an Essay | 112 |
| Appendices | | Writing Tools | 122 |

# CHAPTER 1　Explanatory Paragraphs

We are going to practice explanatory paragraphs. This kind of paragraph explains a topic or expresses an idea on that topic. We will look at paragraph structure and topic sentences. We will also learn some rules of capitalization.

## Part 1　Introduction

▶ Let's use **Model 1** to learn how to write **explanatory paragraphs** one step at a time.

1. Quickly read the paragraph.
2. Discuss what it is about in a group.

### Model 1

**The Benefits of After-school Sports Clubs in Japan**  02

　After-school sports clubs contribute to Japanese students' education in many ways. First, sports clubs teach students lessons in responsibility. Next, sports clubs can help students improve their social skills. Finally, sports clubs also teach students how to take care of their bodies. In conclusion, the lessons that students can learn from their sports clubs help them become more capable adults.

*Notes*

contribute to ... 貢献する、役に立つ　　teach somebody lessons in ... 人に…を教える
social skills ソーシャルスキル、社会的技能　　capable adult 有能な大人

MEMO

▶ Look at Model 1 again and fill in the blanks with appropriate words to see how this paragraph is structured.

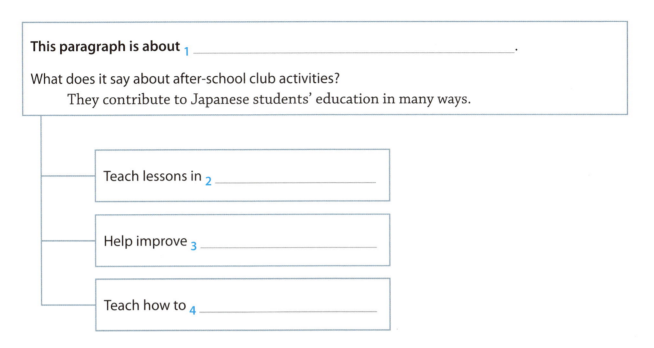

| This paragraph is about ₁ _____. |
| What does it say about after-school club activities? |
| They contribute to Japanese students' education in many ways. |

- Teach lessons in ₂ _____
- Help improve ₃ _____
- Teach how to ₄ _____

## Part 2 — Structure

### Topic sentence

The first sentence of a paragraph is called the **topic sentence**. It is the most important sentence in the paragraph because it <u>tells us two very important pieces of information</u>:

| The topic | The main idea |

<u>After-school sports clubs</u> contribute to Japanese students' education in many ways.
    ↑ the topic              ↑ the main idea

The topic sentence tells us **what to expect in the rest of the paragraph**.

## PRACTICE A

Look at these topic sentences. Circle the topic and underline the main idea for each. 1 and 2 are done for you.

1. (Team sports) are a great way to build stronger relationships.

2. There are many things we can do to fight (global warming).

3. Certain characteristics are required to be a good leader.

4. Having a dog as a pet can help you live a happier life.

5. Smoking can lead to various health problems.

## PRACTICE B

Look at the sentences. Some of them are good topic sentences, but others are not because they are too general or too specific. Mark ○ for good ones and × for bad ones. 1 is done for you.

1. ___×___  I like sports.
2. _____  Daily physical exercise is good for three main reasons.
3. _____  Also, volunteering can teach people how to cooperate with others.
4. _____  There are various kinds of service dogs at work.
5. _____  Students from different cultures come to this university.

## PRACTICE C

Complete the following topic sentences by adding a topic or a main idea. 1 is done for you.

1. Climbing a mountain *can be difficult* for many reasons.

2. Eating junk food every day causes _____.

3. There are _____ to improve your English.

4. _____ are necessary for most courses in college.

5. University cafeterias serve _____.

## Part 3 Writing Tools

## Capitalization

▶ Let's use **Model 2** to learn how to use **capital letters**.

1. Quickly read the paragraph and discuss what it is about.
2. Underline words that begin with a capital letter.

### Model 2

**The Roles of Local Sports Associations**

Local sports associations support local sports clubs in various ways. In Hokkaido, for example, the local sports association holds workshops for sports clubs. They also help local sports clubs to hold events together or with the Japan Sports Association four times a year. In addition, they collect and send out information on sports instructors. To sum up, sports clubs in local communities can develop, hold large events, and share information thanks to the support of local sports associations.

*Notes*
sports association 体育協会　　Japan Sports Association 日本体育協会　　local 地域の　　To sum up, まとめると　　thanks to … …のおかげで

● **Some rules of capitalization**

| Sentence beginning |
|---|
| Local sports ... 1 _____ |
| 2 _____ also .... |
| 3 _____ 4 _____ |

| Names of places, people, and groups |
|---|
| **Places:** Tokyo, New Zealand, Chicago, Paris, 5 _____ |
| **People:** Miyazaki Hayao |
| **Groups:** 6 _____ |

● **Basic capitalization for titles**

Capitalize the initial letter of every word in a title except prepositions and articles. When a title starts with an article, the first letter of the article is capitalized.

▶ Look at **Model 2** again. Write the words you underlined in the title and the paragraph in the appropriate boxes above.

## Part 4 Writing

**PRACTICE D**

There are five errors in the following paragraph. Correct them. Fill in the blanks below with appropriate words to see how this paragraph is structured. Then write a topic sentence.

### New ways Of Communication

_____

_____ .

first, smartphones allow us to see and hear the people we want to talk to anywhere in the world In addition, we can use translation apps on smartphones to help us communicate with people who speak different languages. finally, using social media apps, smartphones help us save memories in pictures and movies in order to share them with a large number of people all at once. To sum up, smartphones allow us new ways to communicate with others that were not available to generations before us.

**Topic:** 1 _____

What does it say about the topic?

2 _____

3 _____

We can use translation apps ...

4 _____

# Brainstorming

When thinking about what to write, brainstorming is one way to generate ideas.

**PRACTICE E**

Brainstorm in pairs or in a group on the following topic. Then write a topic sentence.

1.

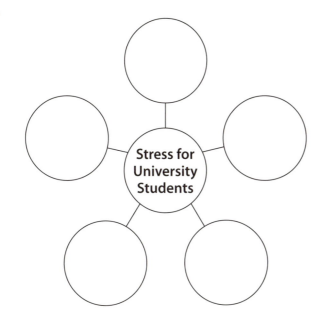

Topic sentence _____

2.

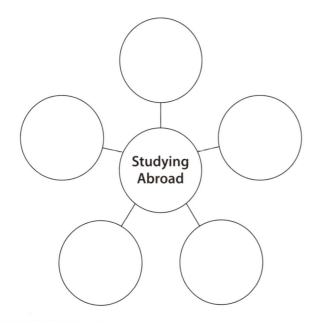

Topic sentence _____

# CHAPTER 2  Information Paragraphs

We are going to practice information paragraphs. This kind of paragraph provides information on a topic in various ways. We will review paragraph structure and learn about supporting sentences. We will also learn basic punctuation rules.

## Part 1  Introduction

▶ Let's use **Model 1** to learn how to write **information paragraphs** one step at a time.

1. Quickly read the paragraph.
2. Discuss what it is about in a group.

### Model 1

**Contact Lenses**  04

　Contact lenses have made the lives of nearsighted people more convenient in several simple, yet very important ways. First, contact lenses give a wider field of vision than glasses. Next, contact lenses make it easier for people who need glasses to play sports. Finally, contact lenses are great for people who like to wear sunglasses. In conclusion, contact lenses help nearsighted people live their daily lives just like people with perfect vision and help us avoid the discomforts caused by wearing glasses.

*Notes*
nearsighted 近視の　　yet それなのに　　a field of vision 視野　　avoid ... …を避ける　　discomfort 不快さ

MEMO

▶ Look at **Model 1** again and fill in the blanks with appropriate words to see how this paragraph is structured.

**This paragraph is about** ₁ _____.

What does it say about **contact lenses**?
They have made the lives of nearsighted people more convenient in several simple, yet very important ways.

- Give ₂ _____

- Make it ₃ _____

- Great for people who ₄ _____

## Part 2  Structure

### Supporting sentences

Once you have announced the topic and main idea of a paragraph, the next step is to <u>support your ideas with reasons</u>. These are called supporting sentences.

> **Reason 1**  **Reason 2**
>
> **First**, contact lenses give a wider field of vision than glasses. **Next**, contact lenses make it easier for people who need glasses to play sports. **Finally**, contact lenses are great for people who like to wear sunglasses.
>
> **Reason 3**

**The supporting sentences support the topic and main idea.**

Signal words such as "**First**," "**Second**," "**Next**," and "**Finally**" are often used to begin supporting sentences.

## PRACTICE A

Read the topic sentence about global warming. Mark ○ for each good supporting sentence and × for the bad ones. Then discuss your reasons. 1 is done for you.

### Topic sentence

There are many things that we can do to fight global warming.

### Supporting sentence

1. __×__ Global warming is a problem that affects everyone on the planet.
   (Reason for × : Doesn't help to fight global warming.)
2. _____ Cleaning the filter can make your air conditioner more efficient.
3. _____ You can make money if you recycle cans.
4. _____ You can save electricity if you do not leave your appliances on standby.
5. _____ Recycling at home can reduce the amount of carbon dioxide that we produce.

## PRACTICE B

Now it's your turn. Write three supporting ideas for the following topic sentence. 1 is done for you.

| Topic sentence | Having a dog as a pet can help you live a happier life. | |
|---|---|---|
| Supporting ideas | 1 | People can enjoy talking with dogs because dogs have the ability to interact with humans. |
| | 2 | |
| | 3 | |

## Practice C

Write a topic sentence and supporting sentences for the following topic.

| Topic | What makes a good leader? |
|---|---|
| Topic sentence | |
| Supporting sentences 1 | |
| Supporting sentences 2 | |

## Part 3　Writing Tools

### Punctuation: Commas

▶ Let's use **Model 2** to learn how to use **commas**.

1. Quickly read the paragraph and discuss what it is about in a group.
2. Circle commas and think about the rules of punctuation.

### Model 2

**Effective Vocabulary Learning**　　05

　There are some important things to consider for effective vocabulary learning. First, decide how much you should study based on your goal and spread out your study sessions evenly. Second, make sure you understand how the words are used in context, not only their meaning. Finally, having an accurate memory is necessary, but how quickly you can recall a word or its meaning is also crucial. In brief, study intervals, collocation information, and recall speed are important for learning vocabulary.

*Notes*

vocabulary learning 語彙学習　　consider 考慮する　　effective 効果的な　　based on ... …をもとに　　spread out 広げる（全体に割り付ける）　　study session 勉強セッション（勉強時間）　　context 文脈　　accurate 正確な　　recall 想起する、思い出す　　crucial 決定的な、不可欠な

● **Comma rules in English are more strict than those in Japanese**

| After signals | First, Second, Finally, |
|---|---|
| Before "and," "but," "so" | Commas did not exist in classic Japanese, but they are used in modern Japanese. |
| because ..., when ..., if ..., although ... | Although Japanese is written both horizontally and vertically, the same Japanese commas are used.<br>When western literature was brought to Japan, commas were introduced into the Japanese writing system.<br>It is said that if the emperor of the Meiji Era had not loved Western novels, there would not have been commas in Japanese writing. |
| Listing | Unlike Japanese, English commas are used before "and," "but," and "so." |

## Part 4  Writing

### PRACTICE D

There are five commas missing in the following paragraph. The first one has been found for you. Find the remaining four, and add one more supporting sentence. Remember to use a signal word.

### Our University

Our university is famous for several amazing features. First of all, the campus is known as the most beautiful campus so neighbors often visit to enjoy it throughout the year. Next the library holds a large number of entries, including audiobooks CDs, and DVDs.

_____

_____

These three features are truly amazing and our university is well-known because of them.

## Chapter 2 — Information Paragraphs

### Practice E

Think about what to write on the following topics. Then, choose one or two topics and fill in the chart. Write a topic sentence and three supporting sentences.

| My Hometown | Tourist Spots | YouTubers |

| Topic | |
|---|---|
| Topic sentence | |
| Supporting sentences — 1 | |
| Supporting sentences — 2 | |
| Supporting sentences — 3 | |

# CHAPTER 3   Opinion Paragraphs

In this unit, we are going to practice opinion paragraphs. This kind of paragraph expresses and explains your opinion on a specific topic. We will continue to review paragraph structure and learn about concluding sentences. We will also learn how to introduce reasons for our supporting ideas.

## Part 1   Introduction

▶ Let's use **Model 1** to learn how to write **opinion paragraphs** one step at a time.

1. Quickly read the paragraph.
2. Discuss what it is about in a group.

### Model 1

**Dinosaur Park 2 Movie Review**  06

    Despite having very famous actors in it, I think that *Dinosaur Park 2* is a terrible movie. First of all, the concept for the movie is ridiculous. Building a dinosaur park was a deadly disaster in the first movie, so why would anyone decide to build another one? Second, I feel that the plot is unbelievable. To stop a big, scary dinosaur from eating everyone, the heroes release an even bigger dinosaur to fight it. Finally, the movie writing is also bad, in my opinion. The only reason there is any drama in the movie is because the characters do not behave like normal people. They make the worst possible decisions, which lead to various kinds of drama. In summary, people should save their money instead of watching *Dinosaur Park 2* because it is unrealistic in many ways.

*Notes*

despite 〜にもかかわらず    terrible ひどい    ridiculous 馬鹿げている    deadly 致命的な    plot プロット・話の筋
behave 行動する    decisions 決断    unrealistic 現実的ではない

MEMO

▶ Look at Model 1 again. Using the key words from Model 1, fill in the boxes to see how this paragraph is structured.

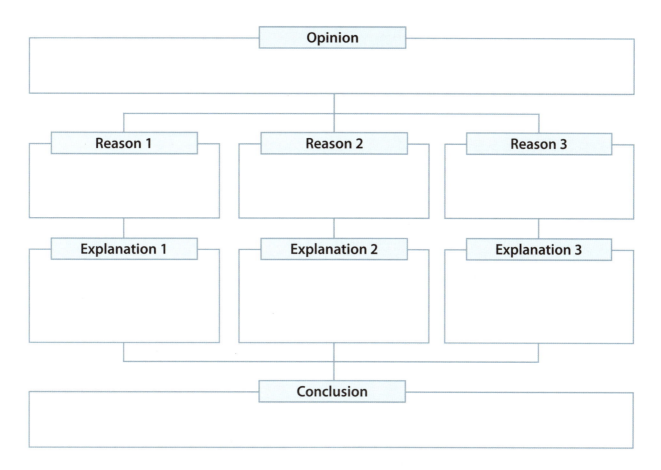

## Part 2  Structure

### Concluding sentence

After you have finished explaining and supporting your opinion, the last step is to finish the paragraph with a **concluding sentence**. This sentence usually summarizes the supporting points or restates the topic sentence using different words.

Signal words, such as "**In summary**," "**In conclusion**," and "**Therefore**," are often used to tell the reader that the paragraph is ending.

## PRACTICE A

Read the topic sentence and choose the sentences that would be good conclusions for the same paragraph. Mark ○ for good examples and × for bad examples. Then discuss your reasons. 1 is done for you.

### Topic sentence

I disagree with the idea that smartphones cause people to communicate less with each other.

### Concluding sentence

1. __×__ In summary, I do not think that smartphones are the best way to communicate.
2. _____ In addition, smartphones allow us to share pictures and videos with friends.
3. _____ In my opinion, smartphones give people the chance to communicate with a larger number of people, faster than ever before.
4. _____ In conclusion, people actually communicate more now than in the past because of smartphones.
5. _____ Therefore, I believe the idea that smartphones are ruining our ability to communicate is wrong.

## PRACTICE B

Read the topic sentence and the concluding sentence. Then, write a check mark to choose the supporting points that would fit in the same paragraph.

| Topic sentence | | I believe that living in the countryside is better than living in the city. |
|---|---|---|
| Supporting sentences | 1. | Many cities in the countryside are famous for different kinds of fruit. |
| | 2. | We can rent larger rooms in the countryside for less money. |
| | 3. | The air is cleaner in the countryside. |
| | 4. | The countryside is usually quiet and peaceful. |
| | 5. | People who live in the countryside usually have to buy a car. |
| Concluding sentence | | In summary, we can live more comfortably in the countryside. |

## Practice C

Write a concluding sentence to match the topic sentence and supporting sentences.

Everyone should try living independently at least once in their life. First, I think that living alone teaches people how to budget their money because they have to pay for their own living expenses. Also, people will not be able to rely on their parents for food, so they will have to learn how to cook by themselves. Finally, in my opinion, people who live independently will learn how to clean as well. They have to do their own chores, such as washing dishes and doing laundry. _____
_____.

## Part 3  Writing Tools

### Expressing opinions and giving reasons

▶ Let's use **Model 2** to learn how to **express opinions** and **give reasons**.

1. Quickly read the paragraph.
2. Discuss what it is about in a group.
3. Circle the key words that express opinions and underline the connecting words that help give reasons.

## Model 2

### Characteristics of a Good Coworker

In my opinion, the three most important characteristics of a good coworker are being responsible, considerate, and helpful. Responsible coworkers will be good team members because they will always do their work thoroughly and on time. In addition, considerate coworkers will not do or say things that disrupt the work environment, so they help everyone work comfortably. Most importantly, I think that coworkers should be helpful to each other. I believe that teams who can rely on each other for help can reach their goals faster. For these reasons, I hope that all of my future coworkers will be responsible, considerate, and helpful people.

*Notes*

characteristics 特徴　　responsible 責任感のある　　considerate 思慮深い　　helpful 助けになる
thoroughly 徹底的に　　disrupt 混乱させる　　rely on ... …に頼る

● **Signals for opinions and reasons**

| Phrases to introduce opinions |
| --- |
| **In my opinion**, P.E. is necessary for three reasons. |
| **I believe/think that** regular exercise helps children develop their physical ability. |

| Words to connect ideas to reasons |
| --- |
| **because** (use before the reason)<br>  I am happy because today is a holiday.<br>  ✕ Today is a holiday because I am happy. |
| **so** (use after the reason)<br>  Today is a holiday, so I am happy. |

### PRACTICE D

Re-write the two separate sentences as one sentence using **because** or **so** where appropriate. Do not rearrange the word order.

1. My father is cooking dinner tonight.  My mother is not feeling well.

2. It is raining outside.  Take an umbrella with you when you leave.

3. I want this party to be a surprise.  Don't say anything to Mariko.

4. Peter is a little nervous.  This is his first time speaking in front of so many people.

## Part 4 — Writing

### PRACTICE E

"Because" and "so" are used incorrectly <u>two</u> times in the following paragraph. Correct them.

---

### Is It Better to Always Tell the Truth?

I believe that telling the truth may not always be the best idea for every situation. First, being completely honest in certain situations might hurt someone's feelings unnecessarily. So telling a small lie can help us avoid this. Second, as long as people are not in any real danger, hiding the truth about something that happened can be a good idea. Because some people panic very easily. Finally, I think it is not wrong to lie about something to protect people. For example, taking the blame for someone else so that they do not get in trouble can be a brave and kind thing to do. In summary, telling a little lie is often a good way of avoiding trouble or hurting other people.

## PRACTICE F

Choose the correct ending to complete each supporting point.

| Topic sentence | I believe that parents make the best teachers for many reasons. |
|---|---|
| Supporting sentences  1. | First, parents spend the most time with their children, so      a) they have more opportunities to teach them.      b) they live together. |
| 2. | Second, parents know what their children should spend time practicing because      a) they know their children's strengths and weaknesses.      b) children can improve faster. |
| 3. | Finally, parents can teach children more about life because      a) the children can be better prepared.      b) they can teach things outside of the classroom. |
| Concluding sentence | In conclusion, children can learn more from their parents than anyone else. |

## PRACTICE G

Choose one of the three topics below and write an outline for an opinion paragraph. Include reasons for each supporting point.

Cats      Homework      School uniforms

| Topic | |
|---|---|
| Topic sentence | |
| Support and reasons  1 | |
| 2 | |
| 3 | |
| Concluding sentence | |

# CHAPTER 4 Descriptive Paragraphs

We are going to practice descriptive paragraphs. This kind of paragraph tells readers about a person, place, or thing. We will also learn how to add more information to supporting sentences.

## Part 1  Introduction

▶ Let's use **Model 1** to learn how to write **descriptive paragraphs**.

1. Quickly read the paragraph without the topic sentence.
2. Discuss what it is about in a group.

---

### Model 1

**Learning Commons**  08

_____. First of all, the area is quite spacious with a high ceiling. The large windows from which you can enjoy the campus scenery also make the space comfortable. Second, it is designed to be convenient for various learning styles. For example, along with a wide, open space that is furnished with tables of different shapes and sizes, there are desks for individual use. Finally, both hardware and software support are available. For instance, access to PCs, printers, and projectors are offered, and experts are stationed for technical support. To sum up, learning commons are increasingly popular among students for their architecture, furnishing, and services.

**Notes**
spacious 広い、広々としている　　ceiling 天井　　furnish 家具を備える　　learning style 学習形態
access to ... …が使える　　station 常駐する

---

MEMO

▶ Look at **Model 1** again.

1. Choose a topic sentence from the choices below.
2. Write the signals (Second, For example, etc.) used.
3. Write the concluding sentence.

| 1. | Topic sentence | a. A learning commons is similar to libraries and classrooms. <br> b. Recently, many universities have learning commons. <br> c. A learning commons is a learning space with several features to benefit students. |
|---|---|---|
| 2. | About the architecture | 1 _____, quite spacious with a high ceiling ... <br> 2 _____ ... |
|  | About the furniture | 3 _____, convenient for various learning styles. <br> 4 _____, .... example/detail |
|  | About the service | 5 _____, both hardware and software supports are available. <br> 6 _____, .... example/detail |
| 3. | Concluding sentence |  |

## Part 2  Structure

### Adding details or examples to a supporting sentence

Once you can write a basic paragraph containing a topic sentence, supporting sentences, and a concluding sentence, the next step is to add more supporting information. There are two ways:

> Give details        Give examples

● **Common signal words**

| To give details | Furthermore, In addition, Additionally, Moreover, In other words, Also |
|---|---|
| To give examples | For example, For instance, such as |

● **Common mistakes!!**

Avoid sentence fragments. When using "For example," you should write a full sentence.

> ✗ I need to take courses to be a P.E. teacher. For example, sports theory and psychology.
> ○ I need to take courses to be a P.E. teacher. For example, sports theory and psychology are compulsory.

## Practice A

For each supporting sentence, choose the additional information that would most likely come next.

### Supporting sentence

1. A solar heating system is installed on the roof. _____
2. The doghouse is designed for a chilly climate, too. _____
3. The living room floor is never freezing. _____
4. Big windows are located on the south side and only small openings on the north side. _____

### Additional information sentence

> A. The walls and floors have extra insulation.
> B. We can enjoy sunlight and warm the rooms on sunny days.
> C. It consists of panels and a tank to store heated water.
> D. There is a radiant heating system installed below the floor.
> E. My dog likes to collect twigs and keep them there.
> F. They are decorated with seasonal stickers.

## Practice B

Choose the best phrase in the parentheses to complete the sentences.

1. The flag of Spain consists of three horizontal bands. ( The bands / The color ) at the top and bottom are red, and the wider center band is yellow.
2. Towards the left side of the center band, there is a coat of arms. ( For example / In detail ), it is a crowned shield, quartered and guarded on each side by the Pillars of Hercules.
3. The center circle of the coat of arms is the emblem of the present Spanish Royal Family, while each quarter shows the badges for the original Spanish Kingdoms. ( For instance / In detail ), the one on the top right is an argent lion with a crown for the Kingdom of León.

## Practice C

Now it's your turn. Write a supporting sentence and write a detail or give an example for the following topic sentence.

| Topic sentence | The attic in my house is my favorite place. |
|---|---|
| Supporting sentence | |
| Detail/Example | |

## Part 3 — Writing Tools

### Descriptive words

▶ Let's use **Model 2** to learn how to use **descriptive words** effectively.

1. Circle the descriptive words.
2. Think about how they are used.

---

### Model 2

**My Favorite Bag**

09

On my twentieth birthday, my grandmother gave me an antique suitcase that became one of my favorites. It is a flap-top travel trunk. She used to go on trips with it on luxurious passenger boats. It is made of smooth brown leather. In addition, the corners are decorated with silver metal pieces. When opened, the inside is fancy, too. Both the bottom and the top parts are lined with print cotton fabric with pockets. For example, one pocket is for keeping shoes, and another is for scarves. The handle is made of soft calf leather and has become softer and more comfortable over the years. Although I do not carry it with me on my trips, I keep my favorite items of clothing in it.

*Notes*
luxurious 豪華な    passenger boat 客船

---

Use various descriptive words so that the reader can imagine what you are describing.

|  | opinion | size→age→shape→color | origin | material |
|---|---|---|---|---|
| a, an, the, these, those, two, 11, 1500 | sweet, sour, salty, spicy, mild, pungent, pleasant, soft, rough | large, long, short, round, square | European, Asian, Japanese | woolen, cotton, wood |

---

### Practice D

Choose the phrase with the correct word order.

1. an Italian expensive leather bag / an expensive Italian leather bag
2. exciting many baseball games / many exciting baseball games
3. 20 sweet large Japanese pears / large sweet 20 Japanese pears

## Part 4  Writing

**PRACTICE E**

There are ten errors in the following paragraph. The first one has been corrected for you. Fix the remaining nine. The highlighted sentence is in the wrong place. Draw an asterisk (*) to show where it should go.

### Crowdfunding
### ~~crowdfunding~~

Crowdfunding is a way to gather monies for a project, and is usually done online. On crowdfunding sites, Small companies, and entrepreneurs are looking for financial support from people around the world. They are developing products, such as games, backpacks, smartwatches. People who give money to these crowdfunding projects are often compensated by receiving the final products at reduced prices. Some of these investor, called angel investors, are looking to buy equity in a company rather than receive products. Furthermore some crowdfunding projects are created to support people in need. Thanks to small donations, Many sick people have been able to continue their lives. Overall people can raise money for various purposes on crowdfunding sites. For example, people donate money when someone needs help paying for medical expenses.

*Notes*
entrepreneurs 起業家　　compensated by 報われる　　equity 株式

## PRACTICE F

Fill in the chart for writing a paragraph on the qualities of a good teacher.

| Title | The Qualities of a Good Teacher |
|---|---|
| Topic sentence | Effective teachers have three qualities in common. |
| Supporting sentences | **About** 1 _____ <br> 2 _____, good teachers are good at developing good relationships with students. <br> Example/Detail **For example,** they gain trust from students because they show how much they trust the students. <br><br> **About** 3 _____ <br> 4 _____, they are compassionate. <br> Example/Detail 5 _____, compassionate people are sensitive to student differences. <br><br> **About** 6 _____ <br> **Finally,** another quality in common is their awareness that learners differ in needs and abilities, and they are able to tailor lessons appropriately. <br> Example/Detail 7 _____, 8 _____. |
| Concluding sentence | 9 _____ |

## Practice G

Discuss in a small group what to write on the following topics. Then, choose one topic and fill in the chart. Finally, write a paragraph. Remember what you have learned so far. Start with a title.

| Successful products/logos | An anime character | _____ for sale |

| | | |
|---|---|---|
| **Title** | | |
| **Topic sentence** | | |
| **Supporting sentences** | About _____ | **First of all,** _____ . |
| | | Example/Detail  **For example,** _____ . |
| | About _____ | **Second,** _____ . |
| | | Example/Detail _____, _____ . |
| | About _____ | **Finally,** _____ . |
| | | Example/Detail _____, _____ . |
| **Concluding sentence** | | |

MEMO

# CHAPTER 5  Comparative Paragraphs

We are going to practice comparative paragraphs. This kind of paragraph explains the similarities between different things. We will also practice words commonly used when making comparisons.

## Part 1  Introduction

▶ Let's use **Model 1** to learn how to write comparative paragraphs.

1. Quickly read the paragraph.
2. Discuss what it is about in a group.

### Model 1

**Comparing American Football and Rugby**  10

People who play American football and rugby will tell you that although their sports have differences, they are actually quite similar in how they are played. First, in American football, the offense tries moving the ball to the other end of the field to carry it over the goal line. Similarly, rugby players are required to run the ball across the field and score points by placing the ball behind the goal line. However, getting the ball to the end of the field is not easy as the opposing teams are looking to tackle players to the ground in both sports. American football and rugby also have similar tackling rules for safety, such as no tripping or pushing from behind. Furthermore, strategy is a big part of both sports. Like the quarterback in American football, the fly-half in rugby navigates their team and knows exactly when to execute a particular game plan. In summary, there are many similarities in the gameplay, rules, and strategy between American football and rugby.

*Notes*
trip 足をひっかける    quarterback アメリカンフットボールのポジション名    fly-half ラグビーのポジション名。国や地域により outside-half, stand-off, first five-eight など異なる名称がある。    execute 実行する

▶▶ Look at Model 1 again and fill in the boxes with key words to see how this paragraph is structured.

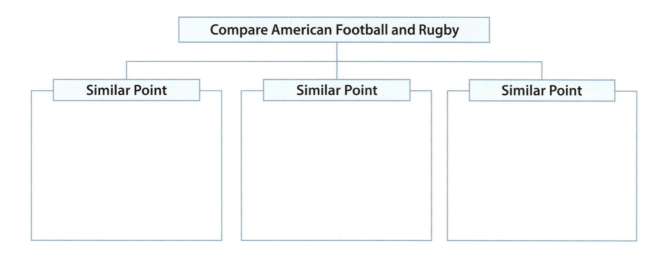

## Part 2　　Structure

## Comparing with a purpose

When you compare two different things, make sure all the points of comparison match with your topic sentences. Your paragraph can change completely based on the controlling idea.

● **Signal words for comparing**

| | | |
|---|---|---|
| **Comparing words** | like | Like soccer, basketball is a sport that requires a lot of physical stamina. |
| | similar to | American football is similar to soccer in that it is also a team sport of eleven players. |
| | both | A balanced diet and regular exercise are both necessary to keep our bodies strong and healthy. |
| | neither | Neither Sakina nor her mother knew how to change the tire, so they asked their neighbor for help. |
| **Comparing sentences** | similarly | If you are trying to lose weight, running is a good way to burn calories. Similarly, swimming is a great exercise that allows you to move your whole body. |

## Practice A

Read topic sentences **A.** and **B.**. Supporting sentences #1~#6 support either **A.** or **B.**. Write A or B in the boxes. Finally, write concluding sentences for **A.** and **B.**.

| | | | |
|---|---|---|---|
| **Topic sentence** | **A.** | Being a student and being a company employee are both equally demanding jobs. | |
| | **B.** | Both students and company employees make efforts to improve their performance. | |
| **Supporting sentences** | 1 | | Like company employees, students have to wake up early every day. |
| | 2 | | Both students and workers ask for help from their peers when necessary. |
| | 3 | | Neither students nor company employees can miss deadlines without penalties. |
| | 4 | | Similar to students, company employees must also work on projects in groups sometimes. |
| | 5 | | Many company workers try to stay motivated by drinking coffee while they work. Similarly, doing homework in cafés helps many students be more productive. |
| | 6 | | Company workers often attend seminars and workshops to improve their skills just like students who study various things. |
| **Concluding sentence** | **A.** | In conclusion, | |
| | **B.** | In summary, | |

## PRACTICE B

Choose the correct comparison word(s).

| like | similarly | both | neither | similar to |

1. Countermeasures against earthquakes in Chile are _____ those in Japan.
2. This is because _____ Japan and Chile are at risk of large earthquakes as they lie on earthquake fault lines.
3. Japan's efforts to prevent earthquake damage include new buildings with quake-resistant designs and older buildings remodeled for better safety. _____, Chile has strict building codes.
4. _____ Japan, Chile has an early warning system to help keep people safe.
5. _____ Japanese nor Chilean research teams are reluctant to share ideas on risk management.

Ring of Fire

## PRACTICE C

Think of two comparison points for similarities between each of the following.

1. The United States and Japan

    a) _____

    b) _____

2. Pizza and pasta

    a) _____

    b) _____

# Part 3  Writing Tools

## Finding the similarities

▶ Let's use **Model 2** to learn how to use comparative expressions effectively.

1. Quickly read the paragraph.
2. Discuss what it is about in a group.

## Model 2

### Christianity and Islam

Christianity and Islam are similar religions in many ways. First, Christians worship only one god, and so do Muslims. In fact, they worship the same god and believe that God created everything in the universe. Second, both religions share many of the same prophets, who are people chosen by God to teach others about God. Like the Bible, Christianity's holy book, Islam's Holy Quran also tells the stories of famous prophets, such as Noah, Abraham, and Moses. Also, Christianity does not hold a belief in reincarnation, and neither does Islam. Both religions teach that our souls are unique to our bodies and that good people are rewarded after death in heaven. In conclusion, Christianity and Islam are not as different as many people believe them to be.

*Notes*

religion 宗教    worship 崇拝する    universe 宇宙    prophet 預言者    Bible 聖書    holy 聖なる
Quran コーラン    reincarnation 生まれ変わり

● **More expressions for comparison**  Watch out for **the word order!!**

| | |
|---|---|
| and ... too<br><br>and so ... | Mariko is allergic to pollen, and Miyuki is allergic to pollen.<br>→ Mariko is allergic to pollen, **and Miyuki is, too**.<br>→ Mariko is allergic to pollen, **and so is Miyuki**. |
| | American football involves physical contact, and rugby involves physical contact.<br>→ American football involves body contact, **and rugby does, too**.<br>→ American football involves body contact, **and so does rugby**. |
| and ... either<br><br>and neither ... | Airplane tickets to Hawaii are not cheap, and tickets to Australia are not cheap, either.<br>→ Airplane tickets to Hawaii are not cheap, **and tickets to Australia are not either**.<br>→ Airplane tickets to Hawaii are not cheap, **and neither are tickets to Australia**. |
| | Mariko has not been to TDL, and some of her friends have not been to TDL, either.<br>→ Mariko has not been to TDL, **and some of her friends have not either**.<br>→ Mariko has not been to TDL, **and neither have some of her friends**. |

## PRACTICE D

Look at Model 2 again. Write below the expressions introduced in the chart on the previous page. Rewrite them as shown in the chart.

1. Christians worship _____
   → (Rewrite) _____

2. Christianity does not _____
   → (Rewrite) _____

## Part 4  Writing

## PRACTICE E

There are eight errors in the following paragraph. Correct them. Write a signal for comparison on the line. Cross out one sentence that is not relevant.

### Quality of life in the U.S. and Japan

The residents of the united states and Japan are very fortunate to live in societies that offer a high quality of life. Although the cost of healthcare in both country vastly differs they are able to offer excellent medical care using the newest medical technology. The average life expectancy of Japanese people was about five years longer than that of Americans in 2017. Because of this, people in both countries can live healthier lives. In addition, Americans enjoy various luxuries, such as shopping malls, concerts, and large sporting events. _____, many Japanese people is able to have fun taking trips abroad during spring and summer vacations. Finally, many kinds of freedom are also available. For example, the U.S. does not have religious restrictions, and neither Japan. For these reasons and many more both the U.S. and Japan are places where people can enjoy a very high quality of life.

## Practice F

Get ready to write a paragraph comparing the similarities between HOUSES and CARS. Brainstorm examples for each of the comparison points. How are both houses and cars similar regarding each point?

| Cost | Example   monthly payments   loan   older ones are cheaper |
|---|---|
| Comfort | Example   functions / facilities |
| Maintenance | Example |

Chapter 5  Comparative Paragraphs

## PRACTICE G

Use your ideas from **PRACTICE F** to write a paragraph comparing HOUSES to CARS. If you would like to compare other things, here are some other topics you can try.

| Topic | Example | Pets and children     Living alone and with family  Schools in Japan and _____ |
|---|---|---|
| Topic sentence | | |
| Comparison points | 1 | |
| | 2 | |
| | 3 | |
| Concluding sentence | | |

39

# CHAPTER 6  Contrast Paragraphs

We are going to practice contrast paragraphs. This kind of paragraph tells readers how certain things are different. We will also learn useful signals and expressions for contrasting.

## Part 1    Introduction

▶ Let's use **Model 1** to learn how to write **contrast paragraphs**.

1. Quickly read the paragraph.
2. Discuss what it is about in a group.
3. Choose an appropriate topic sentence from a, b, and c.

### Model 1

**Running or Walking**  12

　You probably think that the harder the training is, the more effective it is. **3.** ( **a.** Running is not good for your health. **b.** You should walk if you want to lose weight. **c.** Here are some differences between running and walking regarding their impact. ) The most significant difference is their intensity. Running is quite intense and somewhat risky to your heart, while walking is a moderate exercise that anybody can enjoy. Second, excessive training, like running every day, may affect your immune system and lead to a higher chance of you becoming ill. For example, people who run faster and longer may suffer from the common cold more often than those who enjoy walking. Finally and surprisingly, vigorous training like running does not contribute to weight loss as much as you would expect. On the other hand, walking combined with appropriate eating habits helps you become fit. All in all, enjoying walking in your neighborhood could be better than intense running.

*Notes*

intensity 強度　　excessive 過剰の　　immune system 免疫機能　　common cold 風邪　　vigorous 激しい

▶ Look at **Model 1** again. The chart below shows the sub-topics and a detail or example that follows in **Model 1**.

1. Write **the signals** used.
2. Circle either **Running > Walking** (running is better) or **Running < Walking** (walking is better).

| Signal & Sub-topic | Signal & Example/Detail | 2. Circle the correct one. |
|---|---|---|
| 1 _____ ... Intensity | (*No signal is used.*) **Running** is quite intense and somewhat risky to your heart. **Walking** is a moderate exercise that anybody can enjoy. | Running > Walking<br>Running < Walking |
| 2 _____ , ... Chance of becoming ill | 4 _____ , **people who run faster** and longer may suffer from the common cold more often than those **who enjoy walking**. | Running > Walking<br>Running < Walking |
| 3 _____ , ... Weight loss | Vigorous training like **running** does not contribute to weight loss as much as you might expect. 5 _____ , **walking** combined with appropriate eating habits help you become fit. | Running > Walking<br>Running < Walking |
| Conclusion | 6 _____ , enjoying **walking** in the neighborhood > **running** seriously. | |

## Part 2  Structure

## Topic sentences for contrasting paragraphs

Your topic sentence must include the **two things** that you are contrasting.
**Model 1** includes some differences between **running** and **walking** regarding their impact.

● **Signal words for contrasting**

| | | |
|---|---|---|
| Contrasting words and phrases | B is different from A. | British English is different from American English in several ways. |
| | A and B differ. | American English and British English differ. |
| | Unlike A, B .... | Unlike British English, American English spells words more as they sound. |
| Contrasting sentences/ clauses | A ..., but B .... | You normally walk into a building on the first floor in America, but this same floor is called the "ground floor" in Britain. |
| | A .... However, B .... | A popular means of transportation is the "subway" in America. However, it is called the "underground" or "tube" in Britain. |
| | A .... On the other hand / In contrast / Conversely / However, B .... | This laptop company offers a five-year warranty. On the other hand / In contrast / Conversely / However, that laptop is covered only for one year. |
| | While A ..., B .... | While laptop A is fast with a large screen, laptop B is small and light in weight. |

## PRACTICE A

Read the contrasting paragraph. Choose and write the appropriate signal words. Think of a title.

| unlike | on the other hand / however | but | while | different from |

_____

Slow muscles are 1_____ fast muscles in several ways. Slow muscles are for long endurance activities, 2_____ fast muscles are for short, fast bursts. Slow muscles are red due to high levels of myoglobin. 3_____, fast muscles are rather white. Slow muscles are not likely to suffer from hypertrophy, 4_____ fast muscles tend to rather often. 5_____ slow muscles, fast muscles are highly glycolytic. For these reasons, slow muscles and fast muscles are not the same.

*Notes*
endurance 耐久力、持久力   myoglobin ミオグロビン   hypertrophy 肥大   glycolytic 糖分解する

## PRACTICE B

Now it's your turn. Complete each sentence based on the given information.

1. In elementary schools in Japan, class size is limited to 40 students or less, while _____
_____.

   ヒント　アメリカ合衆国では 20 ～ 31 人

2. Some research shows no relation between class size and student achievement, but most researchers have found that children _____
_____.

   ヒント　少人数学級の方が成績が良い ( smaller / better grades )

3. In small classes, children may receive more attention from the teacher. In contrast, _____
_____.

4. Although smaller class size may only have a minor impact on younger children, _____
_____.

5. Unlike classes in Japan, class sizes in the US _____ across the United States.

## Chapter 6 — Contrast Paragraphs

### PRACTICE C

Write two different points for the following topic using the contrasting phrases from **Part 2**.

| Topic | vegan and vegetarian |
|---|---|
| Different points ① | |
| Different points ② | |

## Part 3  Writing Tools

### Adjectives for telling the difference

▶ Let's use **Model 2** to learn how to use comparative words effectively.

1. Quickly read the paragraph.
2. Circle comparative words. The first one is done for you.

### Model 2

**Deciding between At-home Care and Residential Care**

At-home care and residential care (differ) in many ways, which should be considered when choosing one. One of the differences is the expense. Even though some modification to your house may become necessary, at-home care is generally less expensive. Next, you would probably feel more comfortable emotionally in your own home than moving into an unfamiliar place. You do not need to change your lifestyle. You can keep doing what you want whenever you wish, including eating or seeing family and friends. Another significant difference is concerning care workers. While different staff members attend to you at a residential care facility, you receive one-on-one support from regular care workers at home. In this way, you may develop a closer relationship with a care worker. In conclusion, these are a few of the emotional and financial differences for you to consider when choosing a place to live for the rest of your life.

*Notes*
at-home care 在宅介護    residential care 施設介護

● **Rules for comparing/contrasting using adjectives and adverbs**

| -er を付ける | y に変えて -ier を付ける | more/less を使う |
|---|---|---|
| fast → faster | easy → easier<br>heavy → heavier<br>happy → happier | more expensive<br>less convenient |

## PRACTICE D

Look at Model 1 and Model 2. Underline the adjectives used for contrasting.

## Part 4　Writing

## PRACTICE E

There are <u>eight</u> errors in the following paragraph. Correct them. Cross out one sentence that is not relevant.

### Gun Control: AUS vs USA

Gun control in Australia and the United States are different in many ways. First, it is more difficult to buy guns in Australia. for example while Australians have to wait 28 days before they can buy guns and must pass strict background checks, Americans in most states does not have to wait and can buy and sell guns free. Second, the number of guns in each country is very difference. While there were about 13.7 guns per 100 people in Australia in 2016 there were 88.8 in the U.S. Some people own guns because they enjoy hunting. Finally, the rate of gun-related violence in the U.S. is much high than that in Australia. Unlike the U.S., which has multiple mass shootings every year, Australia has had zero since 1996. In summary there are significant differences in gun laws, ownership, and gun violence between Australia and the United States.

*References*
Countries with the most guns, CBC News, Reutors (2016). Retrieved from **http://www.cbc.ca/news/world/small-arms-survey-countries-with-the-most-guns-1.3392204** on May 1, 2018
Australia—Gun Facts, Figures and the Law. Retrieved on May 1, 2016, from **http://www.gunpolicy.org/firearms/region/australia**

*Notes*
multiple 複数の　　mass shooting 銃乱射事件　　ownership 所有

## PRACTICE F

Work in a small group. Follow the steps to complete a paragraph. Decide what to write about. Example topics are given. Prepare questions for collecting information. Interview people, go to the library, or search over the Internet. Then, fill in the chart on the next page.

### Example

| Topic | | |
|---|---|---|
| Number of school days in Japan and the U.S. | | |
| **Main Point** | **Japan** | **USA** |
| **1: school days / week** <br><br> Q1 How many days a week did you go to school? | 6 days | 5 days |
| **2: vacation** <br><br> Q2 When and how long did you have vacations? | July/Aug 40days, 10 days, Dec/Jan,.. | Mid-June, July, August, winter holidays, Easter holidays |

### Topic examples

- different celebrations
- different greeting customs
- public and private school
- team sports and individual sports
- living in an apartment and in a house
- eating out and eating at home
- school uniforms and plain clothes
- going shopping and shopping online

MEMO

Your Chart

| Topic | | |
|---|---|---|
| | | |
| **Main Point** | | |
| **1:** _____<br>Q1 | | |
| **2:** _____<br>Q2 | | |
| **3:** _____<br>Q3 | | |

## Chapter 6 — Contrast Paragraphs

### PRACTICE G

Write a contrasting paragraph based on the information from the activity in **PRACTICE F**.

# CHAPTER 7  Cause and Effect Paragraphs

We are going to practice cause and effect paragraphs. This kind of paragraph explains the reasons for a specific situation. We will also learn conjunctions to express cause and effect.

## Part 1    Introduction

▶ Let's use **Model 1** to learn how to write **cause and effect paragraphs**.

1. Quickly read the paragraph.
2. Discuss what it is about in a group.

### Model 1

**Brain Injuries in Professional Sports**  14

　Professional sports may be connected in several ways to a brain disease called chronic traumatic encephalopathy (CTE). First, CTE can occur due to concussions and repeated impacts to the head. In sports such as American football, rugby, and boxing, head injuries are very common. Because of repeated head injuries like these, players may suffer from behavior problems, memory problems, or dementia later in life. Another possible cause of CTE is athletes returning to their sport too soon after a concussion. Unfortunately, some eager athletes try to hide their symptoms in order to get back into the game. As a result, their bodies do not heal completely, and they increase the risk of long-term damage. Finally, CTE may also be caused by normal gameplay using the head. For example, soccer players are expected to head soccer balls regularly. Although the players do not actually get injured during the game, heading the ball can cause minor damage that builds up over time. For these reasons, some professional athletes suffer from silent injuries long after they have stopped playing.

*Notes*
chronic traumatic encephalopathy (CTE) 慢性外傷性脳症　　concussion 脳しんとう　　impact 衝撃
dementia 痴呆　　eager 熱心な　　symptom 症状

▶ Look at **Model 1** again and fill in the boxes to show how this model is structured.

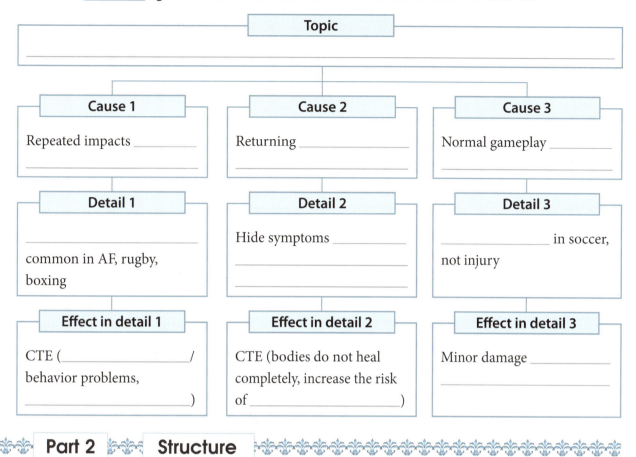

## ❦ Part 2 ❦ Structure ❦

## Topic sentences for cause and effect paragraphs

The **topic sentence** introduces the **result**, **effect**, or **current situation**, and the body of the paragraph explains the **causes** for this.

● **Signal words for telling causes and effects**

|  | Signal words |  |
|---|---|---|
| **Adverb/ Adverbial phrases** | therefore/thus/ consequently | The student seldom came to class and missed many of the assignments. Therefore, it was no surprise that he failed the course. |
|  | for this reason | The roads in mountain towns become icy and slippery during the cold winter season. For this reason, many larger vehicles can be seen with chains covering their tires. |
|  | as a result | The number of children in each of the schools continued to decrease. As a result, the schools had no choice but to close two of the campuses and combine their students. |
| **Clauses** | because/since | Since it is raining, I have decided not to go jogging today. |
| **Phrases** | because of | Many university graduates say that the first two years in their companies are the toughest because of the long hours they have to work. |
|  | due to | Due to the strong winds and heavy rains caused by the typhoon, all of the fireworks festivals were cancelled last weekend. |

49

## Practice A

Fill in the blanks with the appropriate cause-and-effect signal word(s). There could be more than one answer.

| due to | for this reason | as a result | since | because of | therefore |

1. It took 45 minutes longer to arrive at my parents house _____ the heavy traffic on the highway.

2. A large portion of the forest was cut down. _____, most of the animals were forced to move to different areas.

3. _____ you never listen to my advice, I'm not going to help you anymore.

4. _____ a design flaw which caused a large number of the batteries to overheat, Samtech Industries was forced to stop selling their most popular smartphone.

5. The value of the Japanese yen has dropped significantly over the last few years. _____, it is more expensive now for Japanese vacationers to travel abroad.

## Practice B

Read the topic sentence and draw a check mark to choose which sentences explain related causes.

| Topic sentence | | There are several reasons why the air in our cities has become more and more polluted over the last 100 years. |
|---|---|---|
| Causes | 1. | The horizon is no longer visible on certain days of the year because of the poor air quality. |
| | 2. | Many trees in the area were cut down to make room for new buildings. |
| | 3. | The dirty air causes health problems for many of the city's residents. |
| | 4. | The number of cars on the streets has continued to increase year after year. |
| | 5. | As the cities continue to grow, so have the number of factories that pollute the air. |

## PRACTICE C

Think of three causes for the following effect.

| Effect | The percentage of unmarried men under 30 is increasing every year. |
|---|---|
| Causes | ① |
| | ② |
| | ③ |

MEMO

## Part 3 — Writing Tools

### Cause and effect expressions

▶ Let's use **Model 2** to learn how to use **cause and effect expressions**.

1. Quickly read the paragraph.
2. Discuss what it is about in a group.
3. Circle the signals.

### Model 2

**Night Jobs**  15

Although late-night jobs are tempting because of their higher pay rate, they are actually the source of many problems for university students. The first problem is the negative effect on students' health. Because students come home very late at night, they are only able to sleep for a few hours before their morning classes begin. Due to this lack of sleep, students always feel tired and get sick more often. Second, late-night jobs cause problems in class performance and attendance. When students do not get enough sleep, they begin to fall behind on their assignments and miss classes. As a result, these students miss chances to learn and even fail their classes. Finally, students who fail are required to repeat classes in order to graduate. This means that they must pay two or three times the tuition cost for the same classes. For this reason, their part-time jobs are actually making their education more expensive. In summary, late-night jobs pay more per hour, but the cost of their negative effects is much higher.

*Notes*
tempting 誘惑がある　　pay rate 給料　　source 原因　　lack 不足　　attendance 出席
fall behind ついていけなくなる　　fail classes 授業を落とす　　tuition 授業料・学費

### PRACTICE D

Look at **Model 2**. Then, fill in the blanks to show the cause and effect relationship.

1. _____ very late → _____
   → lack of sleep → _____ / get sick

2. Not enough _____ → fall behind on the assignments / _____
   → miss chances to learn / _____

3. Fail classes → required _____ to graduate → must pay more tuition
   → more expensive

52

## Part 4 Writing

**PRACTICE E**

There are ten errors in the following paragraph. Correct them. Write an appropriate signal for the concluding sentence. Cross out one sentence that is not relevant.

### Habitat for Humanity

Habitat for Humanity is a non-profit organization that helps create better living standards for the poor in many developing nation. They help communities build safe and affordable housing, which benefits families and their communities on multiple levels. First having a comfortable house to live in creates a foundation for a happy life. Since a stable house provides shelter from harsh weather, a clean place to live, and a safe place to rest families can focus on work and education instead of constantly worrying about their health or safety. In addition habitat for humanity programs strengthen bonds within communities. As part of their repayment for receiving a new home, families are required to help build houses for other people, too. Because of this system of cooperation the number of people working together in their communities continues to grow. However, building houses by ourselves is difficult in Japan. Furthermore, Habitat for Humanity has a positive effect on international relations. Much of the labor are done by volunteers who come from various countries around the world to work side by side with the locals. As a result many new friendships are made and local businesses also benefit from the tourism boost. _____, Habitat for Humanity programs bring communities and countries closer together and give low-income families a chance for a better life.

*Notes*
affordable 入手可能な　　foundation 基礎　　stable 安定した　　harsh 過酷な　　locals 地域住民
tourism boost 観光業の急成長　　low-income families 低所得家庭

## Practice F

Get ready to write a paragraph explaining the causes of a current social problem. Brainstorm current issues with your class. Then, choose one and write the causes of the problem in the outline below.

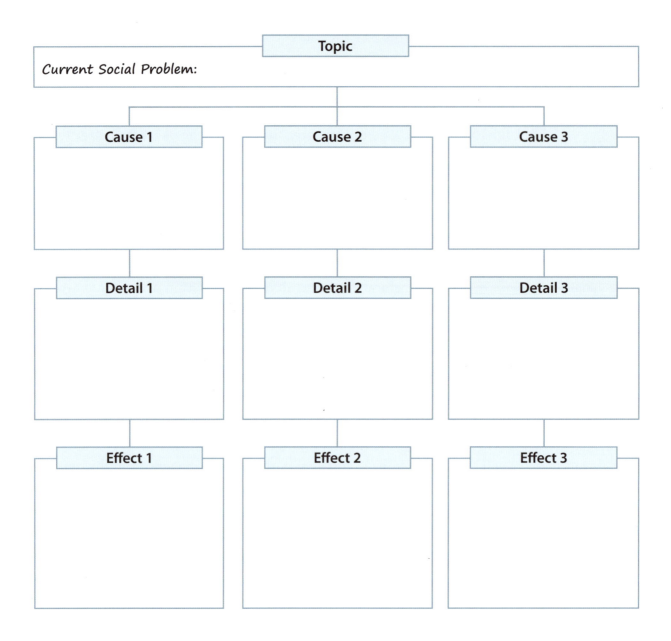

## Practice G

Write a paragraph explaining the causes of a current social problem based on the outline in **Practice F**.

# CHAPTER 8  Argumentative Paragraphs

We are going to practice argumentative paragraphs. This kind of paragraph clearly gives different views, including counter-arguments. We will also learn to provide evidence using references.

## Part 1  Introduction

▶ Let's use **Model 1** to learn how to write **argumentative paragraphs**.

1. Quickly read the paragraph.
2. Discuss what it is about in a group.

### Model 1

**Essential Body Fat**  16

    Although some people exercise regularly to reduce their body fat, having too little body fat is also a problem. Data shows that fashion models are pressured into having strict weight control, which often triggers eating disorders. In fact, some countries, including the USA and Italy, have banned the employment of underweight fashion models. Similarly, some athletes lose weight to be successful in their sports. However, athletes who have reduced weight are likely to suffer from fatigue fractures. This is because they do not have enough estrogen produced from fat cells to increase bone density. As such, research has shown that we need appropriate amounts of body fat cells. The fat cells produce hormones necessary to repair blood vessels and suppress appetite so that we can feel full with less food. In conclusion, while there are legitimate reasons to lose weight, we should avoid excessive weight loss, and we should maintain appropriate body fat levels to stay fit.

*Notes*
underweight 低体重の  eating disorder 摂食障害  ban 禁止する  fatigue fracture 疲労骨折
estrogen エストロゲン  bone density 骨密度  blood vessels 血管  suppress appetite 食欲を抑える

▶▶ Look at Model 1 again and fill in the boxes to show how this model is structured.

**1.** Circle the author's opinion.
   a. If we want to stay fit, we should reduce our body fat.
   b. We all need a certain amount of body fat to stay healthy.
   c. Fashion models and athletes should have little body fat.

**2.** Complete the following outline.

| Point of argument | | Evidence 1 | 3 _____ : suffer from eating disorders |
|---|---|---|---|
| 1 _____ is a problem. | | Detail | Underweight fashion models banned. |
| | | Evidence 2 | 4 _____ : Fatigue fracture |
| Counter argument | | Detail | Lack of estrogen that makes bones stronger |
| Exercise to 2 _____ . | | Evidence 3 | Necessary body fat |
| | | Detail | Hormones from fat cells repair blood vessels and suppress appetite. |

## Part 2   Structure

## Topic sentences for argumentative paragraphs

Your topic sentence(s) must tell **your opinion** (and **the opposing opinion**).

▶▶ Look at Model 1. Circle "**for**" or "**against**" in the parentheses.

> The author is ( for / against ) decreasing body fat, although some people exercise because they are ( for / against ) decreasing body fat.

● **Signal words for evidence**

| For & against | Proponents/Opponents argue that … |
|---|---|
| | Supporters / People who [are for/against, agree/disagree] |
| Contrasting sentences/ clauses | while, although |
| | On the other hand, In contrast, Conversely, However |
| Referencing | According to …, Some people [argue, claim, state, believe] that … |
| | It has been found/reported that …, Studies have found that …, Research shows that …, Data shows … |

## Practice A

Write opinions for and against the following topics.

1. **Topic**  **School uniforms**

   **For**  Students who agree to wear school uniforms say _____
   _____

   **Against**  Those who disagree argue that wearing the same uniform makes students lazy.

2. **Topic**  **Elderly drivers**

   **For**  Proponents state that advanced car safety devices support safe driving.

   **Against**  _____
   no technology can respond to every situation.

## Practice B

Now it's your turn. Complete each sentence with signal words. Number the sentences to form an argumentative paragraph. Think of a title.

| another | some studies show | although | however | despite |

_____

_____ a. _____ the tradition, which is said to have begun in London tube stations, we should consider standing on escalators for transport efficiency and passenger safety.

_____ b. The escalator carried 2500 people per hour when people kept walking on one side. _____, under a stand-only condition, it carried 3500 people.

_____ c. Some of them need to hold on to the rails on both sides, which makes it difficult to stand on a particular side.

_____ d. _____ that walking on one side of an escalator is not always efficient.

_____ e. _____ problem has been raised from physically challenged people.

_____ f. _____ in some countries, including Japan, people stand on one side of escalators to leave the other side open for walkers, this may not be a good practice.

*Reference*
April 6, 2017, on Page A21 of the New York edition with the headline: Why You Shouldn't Walk on Escalators.

58

## Practice C

Write a topic sentence on the opposing opinion for the paragraph in **Practice B**.

_____

_____

## Part 3　Writing Tools

### Expressing opinions of both sides

▶ Let's use **Model 2** to learn how to use signal words effectively.

1. Quickly read the paragraph.
2. Discuss the opposing opinions.

## Model 2

**Genetically Modified Crops**

　Whether to apply genetic engineering on crops is controversial. Proponents argue that some crops should be genetically modified so that they are resistant to rot and pests. This way, farmers do not need to worry about unstable yields. Moreover, some crops can be grown in areas where it used to be difficult to do so. Another advantage of the technology is highly nutritious products. One good example is rice and sweet potatoes containing more vitamin A. These products saved a lot of people in developing countries from vitamin A deficiency, which may cause problems including blindness and limited growth. Opponents, however, are concerned with the possible dangers. Because genetically modified crops are still relatively new, we still do not know of the long-term effects, or if those crops are truly safe. To conclude, although we may need to be aware of the hidden risks, genetic engineering seems to offer great benefits to both agriculture and human well-being.

*Notes*
genetic 遺伝子の　　genetically 遺伝子的に　　modified 操作された　　crops 作物
proponent/opponent 賛成者／反対者　　resistant to ～に耐久性のある　　pest 病気　　yield 収穫量
nutritious 栄養価が高い　　vitamin A deficiency ビタミンＡ欠乏症　　engineering 工学

## PRACTICE D

Look at **Model 2**. Circle the signal words. Analyze the paragraph structure and complete the chart.

| Pros | Resistant to rot and pests, grow in difficult places, highly nutritious products | Stable 2 _____ <br> 3 _____ : Contain more vitamin A |
|---|---|---|
| Cons | 1 _____ | Don't know long term effects <br> Don't know if truly safe |

## Part 4   Writing

## PRACTICE E

There are <u>eight</u> errors in the following paragraph. Correct them. Add signals, if appropriate. Cross out one sentence that is not relevant. Complete the outline below.

---

### Robot Care workers

Have you ever thought about robots taking care of you Some people strongly oppose to having robots replacing nurses or care workers. Robotic technology, however will be of help in aging societies. One example, of such a robot is RIBA, developed in japan in 2009. It was the first robot able to carry a human body from a bed to a wheelchair. The robot looked like a bear. More recently the Telenoid robot was developed in Japan, too. It is equipped with a microphone and a camera to enable remote communication. According to the nursing home staff interaction with this robot have brought emotion back to elderly people. Other developments in the field of robotics, IT, and AI have already been introduced to lessen the burden of nursing. To sum up, these are just a few examples of how robot care workers are helping to assure the wellbeing of elderly people.

*Notes*
IT: Information Technology    AI: Artificial Intelligence

## OUTLINE

| Point of argument | Evidence 1 | 3 _____, Japan, 2009 |
|---|---|---|
| Robotics will be of help 1 _____. | Detail | The first robot to 4 _____. |
| **Counter argument** | Evidence 2 | The 5 _____ robot, Japan |
| Opposed to robots taking care of people instead of 2 _____. | Detail | A 6 _____ and a 7 _____ 8 _____ communication. The interaction has brought 9 _____ back to the elderly. |
| | Evidence 3 | Developments in robotics, IT, and AI |
| | Detail | Lesson burden of 10 _____ |
| | Conclusion | Assure 11 _____ of the elderly |

### PRACTICE F

Work in a small group. Follow the steps to complete a paragraph. Look at Example below. Are you for or against? Write some more reasons. Next, decide what to write about. Use brainstorming to generate ideas (see **Chapter 1**). Go to the library or search over the Internet to find evidence. Then, fill in the chart.

### Example

| Topic | School hours |
|---|---|
| Point of argument | Fewer school hours is better. |
| For or Against | |

| Reasons | For | Children and teachers may be able to rest. Children could attend activities outside of school to develop social skills. More time does not mean more learning. |
|---|---|---|
| | Against | Parents need to come home earlier. Children can enjoy various activities in a safe school environment. Academic performance may drop. |

61

### Example topics

Men should be equally allowed to take parental leave.
More people should live in local towns.
Education should be free for everybody.
Which languages are worth learning?
Children should try various sports.

### Your chart

| Topic | |
|---|---|
| Point of argument | |
| For or Against | |

| Reasons | For | |
|---|---|---|
| | Against | |

## Practice G

Write a paragraph based on the information obtained in **Practice F**.

# CHAPTER 9  Problem and Solution Paragraphs

We are going to practice problem and solution paragraphs. This kind of paragraph introduces a problem and solutions for it. We will also practice using the auxiliary verbs "could" and "would".

## Part 1    Introduction

▶ Let's use **Model 1** to learn how to write **problem and solution paragraphs**.

1. Quickly read the paragraph.
2. Discuss what it is about in a group.

### Model 1

**The Shrinking Countryside**  18

As more Japanese people move to large metropolitan areas such as Tokyo and Osaka, rural towns will continue to shrink. Here are some ideas to address this issue. Some experts have suggested that rural towns could promote immigration by offering immigrants work or inviting them to start businesses. Another solution may be tourism. Improving tourism could be an opportunity for rural towns to create jobs and increase the population. As a result, young people may choose to work in the tourism industry instead of moving to a bigger city. Finally, while immigration and tourism can help rural populations, stopping families from leaving these towns is the most critical issue. Living cost discounts or benefits for families may stop them from moving out. Providing better living conditions for residents and inviting immigrants and tourists could save rural towns from decreasing populations.

*Notes*
metropolitan area 都会   immigrants 移住者   tourism 観光産業   critical 重要な   residents 住民

▶ Look at Model 1 again and fill in the boxes with key words to show how this paragraph is structured.

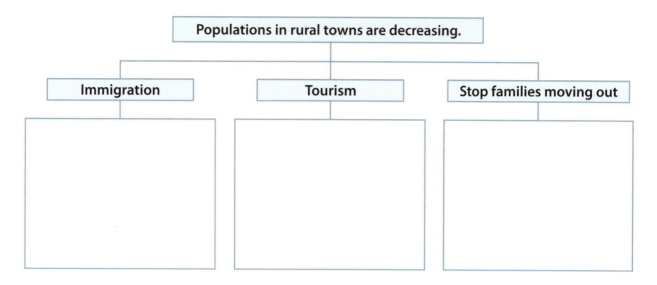

Part 2    Structure

## The structure of problem and solution paragraphs

1. Introduce and explain the problem.
2. Offer a few solutions.
3. Explain the possible results of these solutions.

● **Auxiliary verbs**

|  | Auxiliary verbs | Examples |
|---|---|---|
| For possibility | can | Unhealthy eating habits can lead to health problems as you get older. |
|  | could | You could suffer from diabetes. |
| For future and hypothetical situations | will | Adding ramps to each entrance will make the building barrier-free. |
|  | may | People in wheelchairs may choose to visit the restaurant. |
|  | would | If someone posted that the restaurant has barrier-free facilities, more people would plan to visit the restaurant. |

65

## PRACTICE A

Read the topic sentence and the effects of the problem, then choose with a check mark the sentences that offer solutions to the problem.

| Topic sentence and effects | | The cities we live in have become more polluted over the last 100 years. The dirty air has begun to block our sky and cause health problems. Also, we are now forced to buy bottled water because our natural water sources have become contaminated. |
|---|---|---|
| Solutions | 1. | Using public transportation instead of private cars would produce less carbon dioxide. |
| | 2. | Even simple measures such as recycling plastic can reduce the amount of garbage dumped into our oceans. |
| | 3. | Leaving your house 20 minutes early will help you avoid the morning traffic in busy areas. |
| | 4. | If people wore masks more often, they would not get sick as much. |
| | 5. | Switching to solar energy will also reduce the waste produced by coal and fossil fuels. |

## PRACTICE B

Fill in the blanks with the correct auxiliary verb.

| can | could | will | would |

1. Moving into a new apartment _____ be very costly nowadays.
2. During the busy season, moving companies _____ try to charge you three or four times their regular rates.
3. If you had moved before the busy season, you _____ not have to pay so much.
4. You _____ save additional money on your rent if you searched for places farther away from the city center.
5. Finally, do not hesitate to ask if prices _____ be lowered.

## Practice C

Think of three possible solutions for each of the following problems.

| Problem | The number of university graduates who quit their new jobs within three years is increasing. |
|---|---|
| Possible solutions | a) |
| | b) |
| | c) |

| Problem | Commuting in the morning is becoming uncomfortable for many people because of crowded trains. |
|---|---|
| Possible solutions | a) |
| | b) |
| | c) |

## Part 3  Writing Tools

### Using verbs as nouns

▶ Let's use **Model 2** to learn how to use **gerunds**.

**1.** Quickly read the paragraph and discuss what it is about with your partner.
**2.** Circle the verbs that are being used as nouns.

### Model 2

**Plagiarism**  19

Plagiarism can be a big problem when writing reports and essays, but there are several things you can do to avoid it. First, if you want to write specific sentences exactly as they were used somewhere else, you could use quotation marks. Putting quotation marks at the beginning and end of your quoted sentence shows that you are borrowing the idea. Make sure to also cite your source by writing exactly where you found the sentence. Second, you can also summarize or paraphrase if you just want to borrow an idea. To do this, just write the information as you understand it, using your own words, without copying the sentences exactly. However, telling the reader where you found the information is necessary for this too. Finally, the most important step in avoiding plagiarism is doing your own work. Even if you are busy or forgot your homework, copying someone else's writing will get you into trouble. Also, if you are struggling because you do not understand something, you can always ask your teacher for help. By clearly showing the sources for your information and never cutting corners, your writing will improve, and your plagiarism worries will disappear.

*Notes*

plagiarism 剽窃   avoid 避ける   quotation marks 引用符（" "）   quote 引用する   cite 参照する
paraphrase 言い変える   cutting corners 手を抜く

● **Gerunds:** Using the "ing" form of a verb as a noun.

| Verb | Gerund | Example |
|------|--------|---------|
| put | putting | **Putting** quotation marks at the beginning and end of your quoted sentence shows that you are borrowing the idea. |
| tell | telling | **Telling** the reader where you found the information is necessary for this too. |
| avoid | avoiding | The most important step in **avoiding** plagiarism is doing your own work. |
| copy | copying | **Copying** someone else's writing will get you into trouble. |

## Part 4  Writing

### PRACTICE D

There are ten errors in the following paragraph. Correct them by changing verbs and gerunds where appropriate. Cross out one sentence that is not relevant.

### Language Learning is Not So Difficult

Learning a second language can be quite challenging and intimidating, but here are three solutions to make language learning easier. Manage your study time is the first step. Set aside 20 or 30 minutes daily will give you plenty of time to study without feeling too busy. In addition, it will be much less stressful for you than cramming before tests. Second, finding a study method you enjoy. For example, if you like movies, watch movies in the language you are learning could be a wonderful opportunity to practice listening and learn new phrases. Some students do not like horror movies. Listen to music during your commute is another fun way to study without feeling like you are actually studying. Finally, starting carrying a small language notebook with you. Write down new and useful phrases that you hear will help you remember them later. Even if you do not understand them at the time, take a quick note could give you the chance to asking questions later. With these quick and easy solutions, learn a second language will be a piece of cake.

*Notes*
intimidating 手ごわい   cram つめこむ

### PRACTICE E

Fill in the blank with the correct word choice by changing it into gerund form.

| exercise | drink | come | see | stare |

1. _____ at your cellphone before bed can make it harder for you to fall asleep.

2. Mike loves sitting by a window and _____ coffee on a rainy day.

3. My favorite part of the trip was _____ the elephants.

4. _____ for 20 minutes five days a week is an easy way to stay in shape.

5. You can't learn a new language just by _____ to class. You have to study, too.

## Practice F

Get ready to write a paragraph that explains a problem and offers solutions. First, try brainstorming current problems. Write as many as you can in the box.

**Current problems**

Ex. too busy for homework

Next, choose three problems, and brainstorm possible solutions for each.

**Problem 1**

Ex. too busy for homework

**Solutions**

Ex. Reduce work hours
Study on the train

**Problem 2**

**Solutions**

**Problem 3**

**Solutions**

Choose one problem, then write a few details about it and write practical solutions for it in the outline below.

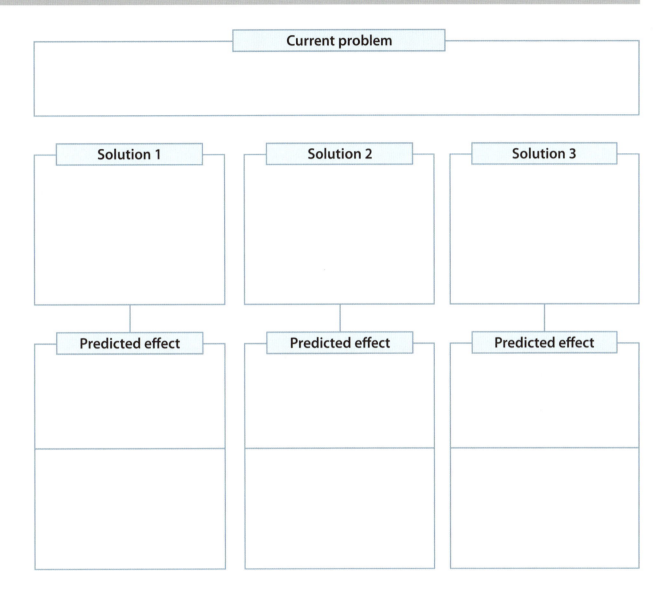

# CHAPTER 10  Time-order Paragraphs

We are going to practice time-order paragraphs. This kind of paragraph narrates events in the order they happened. We will learn expressions to clarify the chronological order of events.

## Part 1  Introduction

▶ Let's use **Model 1** to learn how to write **time-order paragraphs**.

1. Quickly read the paragraph.
2. Discuss what it is about.

### Model 1

**Goalball**  20

　Goalball is a team sport for visually impaired people. Two teams of three members compete to roll a ball past their opponents and into the goal. Although all players wear a black eyeshade to equalize their blindness, they can track the ball by the sound of two bells inside. Goalball has spread worldwide in a relatively short span of about 70 years. According to the International Blind Sports Federation, goalball was originally invented by an Austrian and a German in 1946 to rehabilitate soldiers who had lost their sight in World War II. Thirty years after its invention, it was approved as an official sport in the Toronto Paralympic Games and has been played in all Paralympic Games since then. Goalball was first introduced to Japan in 1982, but it was not very popular until the rules were translated into Japanese in 1992. Then, introductory lessons started to be offered in several para-sports centers. In 2004, the first Japanese women's team participated in the Paralympic Games in Athens and won bronze medal. Since then, the women's team has participated in four Paralympic Games—in Athens, Beijing, London, and Rio de Janeiro. Naturally, thanks to this consecutive participation, goalball has now become the most popular it has ever been in its history.

**Notes**
visually impaired 視覚障がい　rehabilitate 機能を回復する　International Blind Sports Federation 国際視覚障がい者スポーツ協会　introductory 初心者　consecutive 連続した

▶ Look at Model 1.
  1. Underline the topic sentence.
  2. Double underline the expression that hints that this paragraph is about events in history.
  3. Circle words and expressions that tell you the order of events.

▶ Complete the outline of the model. The beginning is done for you.

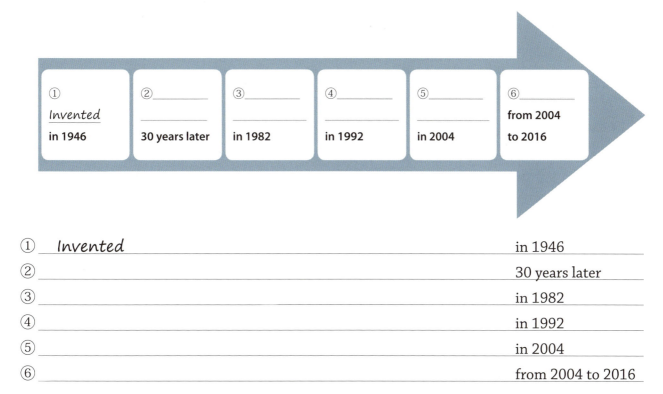

① _Invented_ _____ in 1946
② _____ 30 years later
③ _____ in 1982
④ _____ in 1992
⑤ _____ in 2004
⑥ _____ from 2004 to 2016

  Part 2  Structure

## Topic sentence & concluding sentence

The **topic sentence** in a time-order paragraph tells the reader that this paragraph will narrate the events that happened.

> Goalball has spread all over the world in a relatively short span of 70 years.

The **concluding sentence** mentions the topic again to remind the readers of the topic.

> Naturally, thanks to this consecutive participation, goalball has now become the most popular it has ever been in its history.

## Supporting sentences

**Supporting sentences** in a time-order paragraph tell the events in order.

| Event 1 | → | Event 2 | → | Event 3 |
|---|---|---|---|---|
| Detail 1 | | Detail 2 | | Detail 3 |

## Practice A

Read these sets of supporting sentences. Then, number the sentences to show the correct order. Write a suitable concluding sentence.

| Topic | | Japanese Sign Language Interpretation |
|---|---|---|
| 1. | Topic sentence | Japanese sign language (JSL) interpretation started nearly half a century ago. |
| 2. | Supporting sentences | _____ |
| 3. | | _____ |
| 4. | | _____ |
| 5. | | _____ |
| 6. | | _____ |
| 7. | Concluding sentence | _____ |

a. Now the quality and professional skill of interpreters is ensured by a national examination.

b. The Japanese government began to support sign language interpretation services several years after the formation of the first study group.

c. Thanks to the "International Year of Disabled Persons" in 1980, demand for professional JSL interpreters increased.

d. Before the 1960s, proficient JSL users, such as sign language teachers and families of deaf members, volunteered as interpreters.

e. When the first sign language study group started in 1963, many other study groups also started all over Japan.

## Practice B

Now it's your turn. Create a story in pairs or groups. Take turns to create sentences. Use at least one time expression in each sentence. The story starts with "Once upon a time."

### A Story of _____

1. Once upon a time, _____
2. _____
3. _____
4. _____

## Chapter 10   Time-order Paragraphs

### Practice C

Write a topic sentence and a concluding sentence for narrating the following topic.

| Topic | Planning a Career |
|---|---|
| Topic sentence | |
| Concluding sentence | |

## Part 3   Writing Tools

### Signals to show time order

▶ Let's use **Model 2** to learn how to use commas.

1. Quickly read the paragraph and discuss the structure with your partner.
2. Underline expressions of time and discuss how they are used.

### Model 2

**Coming-of-Age Ceremony**

   Emi attended the Japanese traditional celebration for turning 20 in January. Her celebration began as early as half a year before the day. In the summer of the previous year, she visited a kimono shop with her mother. They spent nearly two hours before deciding on one set of kimono and obi. On the way home, Emi made a reservation with a hairdresser and kimono dresser for the day at 7:30 because she would have to leave there for the ceremony by 9 o'clock. Two weeks later, she went back to the shop to pick up her kimono. She would never forget how excited she was. For nearly six months, she enthusiastically worked out, dreaming of herself in the beautiful kimono. Finally, the day came. Emi left home at 6 o'clock to get her hair done and get dressed. Two hours later, her mother picked her up at the hairdresser's to drive her to the ceremony venue. When she got there, there were many of her former classmates, all very cheerful. After the ceremony, which lasted one and a half hours, she went to a reunion party and had a great time. The celebration for turning 20 turned out to be one of the best memories of her life, preparation and all.

*Notes*
enthusiastically 熱心に   venue 開催地   former 以前の   lasted 続いた   a reunion party 同窓会

Signal words to show time are essential for narration. Prepositions to show time or a time frame are also useful.

● **Comma rules**

|   | Subordinators |
|---|---|
|   | *When* you give your mouse a cookie, he will ask for more. |
| a. | *Before* he finishes another cookie, he asks for milk. |
| b. | *When* he finishes his cookie, he asks for more. |
| c. | *When* the woman sits in the kitchen at night, the mouse shows up. |
| d. | *Until* the mouse is satisfied, the woman usually stays with him. |
| e. | *Since* the woman started living in this house, she has enjoyed time with her friend. |
| f. | *By the time* the woman gets sleepy, the mouse will be satisfied. |
| g. | *While* he eats the cookie, he thinks about asking for more. |
| h. | *As soon as* the mouse sees her, he asks for a cookie. |

(From "If You Give a Mouse a Cookie")

|   | Prepositions |
|---|---|
| a. | *In* summer school, children go into the woods to look for stag beetles very early in the morning. |
| b. | *During* summer vacation, some children attend summer school in rural areas. |
| c. | Some children are invited to the Sunday school at a nearby church *on* Sunday mornings.<br>× ... *in* Sunday morning |
| d. | The experience of living in a different environment will mean something later *in* the children's life. |
| e. | *Before* coming to the village, most children are worried whether they can adjust to the local life. |
| f. | *For* more than ten years, a small village has been accepting children from large cities to its summer school. |

## Practice D

Put the sentences in the box on page 76 in the correct order.

Subordinators

| 1. e | 2. | 3. h | 4. | 5. | 6. a | 7. | 8. f |

Prepositions

| 1. | 2. f | 3. | 4. a | 5. | 6. |

## Part 4 — Writing

## Practice E

There are eight errors in the following paragraph. Correct them. Complete the concluding sentence.

### Wooden bowl (Folktale)

The other day my roommate told me a folktale about a little boy who lived with his parents and his grandfather. As far as the boy could remember the family used to gather at the dining table and enjoyed every meal. However, as the grandfather grew older he started to lose control of his hands and arms, often spilling food. Soon after, the boy's parents decided to have his grandfather eat at a separate table, alone. The grandfather was fed his food in a wooden bowl. one day, the little boy was carving something out of a block of wood in the backyard. When his father asked what he had been making he replied, "A wooden bowl for you and mother to use when you get older." At the very next meal the _____

_____ as they used to.

## Practice F

Think about what to write for the following topics. Write an outline and a topic sentence.

| Birthday party | Biography of favorite actor/actress | A historical event |

| | | |
|---|---|---|
| **Topic** | | |
| **Topic sentence** | | |
| **Supporting sentences** | Event | |
| | Detail | |
| | Event | |
| | Detail | |
| | Event | |
| | Detail | |
| **Concluding sentence** | | |

## Practice G

Write a paragraph based on your outline in **Practice F**.

# CHAPTER 11  Process Paragraphs

We are going to practice process paragraphs. This kind of paragraph tells how to do something. We will learn to write clear, step-by-step instructions using signals effectively.

## Part 1    Introduction

▶ Let's use **Model 1** to learn how to write **process paragraphs**.

1. Quickly read the paragraph.
2. Discuss what it is about in a group.

## Model 1

### Earthquake Safety Procedures at Home  22

When a big earthquake strikes, it is important to take appropriate action. First, duck where you are, covering your head and neck with your arms. If a table or desk is nearby, get under it for shelter and hold onto its legs. If no shelter is nearby you, move to an inside corner of the room. Do not move to another location or outside yet. Stay there until the shaking stops. When it stops, be sure to turn off all stoves and heaters. Do not forget to put on shoes to protect against sharp objects such as broken glass. Finally, evacuate on foot if possible. Walk carefully out of the building, check the safety of your own house, and go to the nearest designated evacuation area. In case of a big earthquake, remember to duck, cover, and hold on for safety.

**Notes**

duck しゃがむ    inside corner 建物内部側の隅    stove 調理用ガスコンロ    evacuate 避難    designated 指定された

MEMO

▶ Look at **Model 1** again.

1. Complete the outline of the model. Some parts of the outline are done for you.
2. Write the signal words used to tell the order.

| Signal word | First |
|---|---|
| Action 1 | Duck where you are and cover your head and neck with your arms. |
| Details | Get under a table for shelter and hold onto its legs. |

| Signal word | Until the shaking stops |
|---|---|
| Action 2 | |
| Details | Do not move to another location yet. |

| Signal word | |
|---|---|
| Action 3 | |
| Details | Do not forget to put on shoes. |

| Signal word | |
|---|---|
| Action 4 | Evacuate on foot. |
| Details | Walk carefully out … |

## Part 2　Structure

### Topic sentence & concluding sentence

**The topic sentence** in a process paragraph tells the reader that <u>this paragraph will give instructions on how to do something</u>. **The concluding sentence** <u>mentions the topic again</u> to remind the readers of the topic.

Topic sentence

<u>When a big earthquake strikes</u>, it is important to take appropriate action.
↓　　　　　　　　　　　　　　↓
<u>In case of a big earthquake</u>, remember to duck, cover, and hold on for safety.

Concluding sentence

## Supporting sentences

Supporting sentences in a process paragraph give step-by-step instructions. Ideally, the steps should be in order.

Event 1 → Event 2 → Event 3
Detail 1 | Detail 2 | Detail 3

**PRACTICE A**

Read the supporting sentences from **a** to **g**. Write a suitable topic sentence. Then, number the sentences to show the correct order. **4** is done for you.

| Topic | Steps to create a shopping account |
|---|---|
| Topic sentence | |
| Supporting sentences | 1. _____ <br> 2. _____ <br> 3. _____ <br> 4. *a* <br> 5. _____ <br> 6. _____ <br> 7. _____ |

a. Receive email.
b. Your account is ready.
c. Input required information and create a password.
d. Input your name and email address to receive an email.
e. Find and click a button to register or create an account.
f. Go to the top page of a shopping website.
g. Click link to the registration page.

## Practice B

Now it's your turn. Look at the memo and write supporting sentences to explain the procedure.

Topic

Required procedure for entering the USA to study

MEMO
*****************************

1. Upon landing follow the directions to "Immigration," and get in the line for "Non-Residents."
2. Immigration officer (passport, I-20)
3. QA, fingerprint, photograph
4. Go to baggage claim

Supporting sentences

#1: _____ landing.

#2: _____ to an immigration officer's counter and _____ your passport and Form I-20.

#3: After several _____, you will be _____.

#4: You can then proceed to the baggage claim area.

## Practice C

Write a topic sentence and concluding sentence for the following topic.

| Topic | Making hotel reservations online |
|---|---|
| Topic sentence | |
| Concluding sentence | |

## Part 3 — Writing Tools

### Punctuation: Commas for signals and clauses

▶ Let's use **Model 2** to learn how to use **commas**.

1. Quickly read the paragraph and discuss the structure with your partner.
2. Underline signal words and think about how they are used.
3. Circle commas and discuss why they are necessary.

### Model 2

**Yoga: The Correct Way of Doing "Bird Dog"**   23

For any kind of coordination training, it is important to focus on correct movement first, rather than quick movement, because accuracy of movement connects your mind and body. The following shows how to do "bird dog" effectively. To begin, get down on all fours. Make sure your hands are under your shoulders, and your knees are under your hips. Your feet should be flexed. First, kick one leg out straight behind you while stretching the other arm out straight forward. Instead of lifting your leg or arm up high, you should try to stretch your arm and leg in opposite directions. Also, tighten your gluteal and abdominal muscles. Next, as you lower your arm and leg, bend them to bring them under your body until your knee touches your elbow. Then, extend them back out. Repeat several times on one side before switching to the other side. Controlled, slow, and correct "bird dog" training will bring better coordination.

*Notes*

coordination 協調　　on all fours 四つ這い　　gluteal muscles 臀筋(でんきん)　　abdominal muscles 腹筋

Signal words such as **first**, **next**, or **finally** are often used to begin supporting sentences. **When/after/before/until/as soon as** clauses are also useful.

● **Comma rules**

| Commas after signals | Commas after subordinate clauses |
|---|---|
| **To begin,** remember that you should enjoy reading. | **If** you are going to be late for dinner, you should text somebody in the family. |
| **First,** try a book of an easy level series and read some more from the same series. | **As soon as** everybody comes home, they start cooking. |
| **Second/Next,** when you can read quite fluently, move on to the next level. | **When** everybody is seated, the dinner starts with a prayer. |
| **Then,** stay at the same level until you become comfortable at the level. | **Until** everybody finishes, you are not supposed to leave the table. |
| | **Before** you leave the table, remember to thank the cooks for the dinner. |

Part 4    Writing

**PRACTICE D**

There are ten errors in the following paragraph. Correct them. Complete the concluding sentence.

### How to wash fresh fruits and vegetables

Fresh fruits and vegetables should be washed appropriately Because they can have pesticides or bacteria on their surface. First remove the original packages or containers just before you are ready to use them. Then, rinse the fruits and vegetables with running water. Be sure not to use cleaners such as soaps or detergents to wash products. If they are not rinse completely you might ingest the residue of the cleaners. Finally pat them with a paper towel to remove wetness. That is all you need to do, you are now ready to cook. It is important _____

_____, but it is that simple!

## Practice E

Think about the procedure for the following topics. Then, choose one topic and write the outline to explain the steps. Start with a topic sentence and end with a concluding sentence.

| Exam Procedure | Submitting Reports | Earthquake Procedure when Driving |

| | | | |
|---|---|---|---|
| **Topic** | | | |
| **Topic sentence** | | | |
| **Supporting sentences** | 1. | | |
| | | 1) | |
| | | 2) | |
| | 2. | | |
| | | 1) | |
| | | 2) | |
| | 3. | | |
| | 4. | | |
| **Concluding sentence** | | | |

86

## Practice F

Write a paragraph based on the outline in **Practice E**.

# CHAPTER 12     Summaries

We are going to practice summaries. This kind of paragraph summarizes the content of an article, report, etc. We will practice finding the main ideas and the details. We will also learn how to avoid plagiarism.

## Part 1     Introduction

▶ Let's use **Sample Article 1** to learn how to write a **summary**.

1. Quickly read the article.
2. Discuss what it is about in a group.

### Sample Article 1

**Child Obesity**  24

    Over the last few decades, changes in American culture and society have caused child obesity to become a serious problem. Culturally, convenience is often a top priority in the United States. This is why you can find fast food restaurants on nearly every street corner from coast to coast. The meals served in these restaurants are usually inexpensive and tasty too, which makes them very appealing. Even though they are almost always unhealthy, busy people and people who do not have a lot of money to spend end up feeding their children fast food four or more times a week. The amount of junk food consumed in American homes has also increased. In the past, children drank a can of soda once or twice a week on average. Now, the average child drinks two cans a day. Unfortunately, it does not end there. Sugary cereals have become the standard breakfast for American children as well. In fact, almost all foods that are advertised on TV targeting children are junk food. To make a bad situation worse, children are also moving much less than they used to. Fewer children are walking to school or playing outside. Most children choose to entertain themselves by watching TV or playing video games. This keeps them sitting on the sofa and severely reduces the amount of exercise they get. In 2017, researchers found that 18.5% of American children were obese, and that number is expected to continue to rise (The State of Child Obesity, (n.d.)).

*Reference*
The State of Child Obesity. (n.d.). Retrieved on March 25, 2018, from https://stateofobesity.org/childhood/

*Notes*
over the last few decades この数十年間　　obesity 肥満症　　were obese 肥満であった　　culturally 文化的に
a top priority 最優先順位　　standard 標準的

▶ Look at **Sample Article 1** again and fill in the blanks with appropriate words to complete the outline of this article.

## Outline

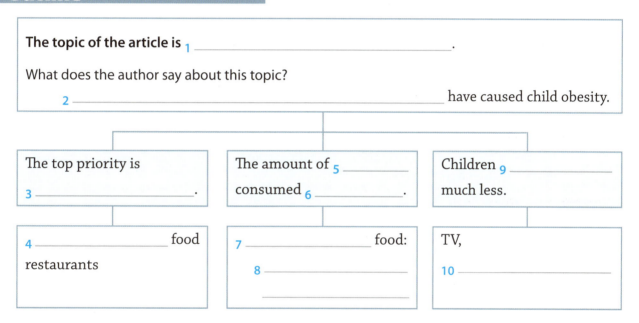

## Part 2　Structure

### Writing a summary

When summarizing, give only main ideas. Details are not necessary.

▶ Look at **Sample Article 1** again and the **outline** you have completed.

The blue boxes show the main ideas that should be included in the summary.

# Part 3 Writing Tools

## Paraphrasing

The sentences in summaries must give the same information as the article, but must be written in a way that changes the style or summarizes the original sentence. This is called **paraphrasing**.

▶ Look at the Example below.

### Example

**Original**
This is why you can find fast food restaurants on nearly every street corner from coast to coast.

**Paraphrasing**
1. ( ✓ ) There are many fast food restaurants in the US.
2. ( ) Fast food restaurants are on every street corner from coast to coast.
3. ( ✓ ) Fast food restaurants are very easy to find in the US.
4. ( ✓ ) Fast food restaurants are extremely popular among Americans.
5. ( ) American fast food restaurants are great.

- Numbers 1, 3, and 4 properly paraphrase the original sentence. They give the same information expressed in different words.
- Number 2 is inappropriate because a large portion, "on every street corner from coast to coast," is copied from the original sentence.
- Number 5 is inappropriate because it gives unrelated information.

### PRACTICE A

Look at the sentences. Put a check mark ( ✓ ) next to sentences that properly paraphrase the selection from **Sample Article 1**. Discuss why each sentence is appropriate or inappropriate.

**1.**

*In the past, children drank a can of soda once or twice a week on average. Now, the average child drinks two cans a day.*

1. ( ) Children used to drink one can of soda a week, but now they drink two cans every week.
2. ( ) Children are now drinking much more soda daily than they did in the past.
3. ( ) Soda drinking among children has increased from twice a week to twice a day.
4. ( ) Before, children drank a can of soda once or twice a week on average. Nowadays, the average child drinks two cans a day.
5. ( ) More children are choosing to drink sodas everyday instead of water.

**2.**

*In 2017, researchers found that 18.5% of American children were obese.*

1. (　) Roughly 1 in 5 American children were considered obese in 2017.
2. (　) According to a study in 2017, most US children are considered to be obese.
3. (　) 18.5 American children were expected to be obese in 2017.
4. (　) In 2017, 18.5% of American children were obese.
5. (　) Obesity among American children has increased to almost 20%.

## Plagiarism

Now that you have practiced paraphrasing, why is paraphrasing necessary?

It is necessary because if you use someone else's writing or ideas as if you had created them, you are "cheating." This is called **PLAGIARISM**. You should always be careful to avoid plagiarism.

### ● Why is plagiarism bad?

When you copy someone else's writing, or use their ideas or research without giving them credit, it is considered to be dishonest. Doing so is like stealing their work. Therefore, students, researchers, and writers of all kinds have to be careful.

### ● How to avoid plagiarism

When using information from other sources, such as books, papers, websites, and news article, you may violate copyrights of the original writers. Be sure to use your own words.

Here is a list of Don'ts:

- **Don't copy word for word.**—Try to write everything in your own words.
- **Don't mix and match data or ideas.**—If you mix data, their sources will become unclear or inaccurate.
- **Don't copy ideas.**—If you are using someone else's idea, you must say whose idea it is.
- **Don't forget to cite sources.**—Write where you found the information so that other people can check the information too.

# Part 4　Writing

▶ Let's use **Sample Article 2** to practice **summary writing**.

1. Quickly read the sample article.
2. Discuss what it is about.

## Sample Article 2

### Recovery of Kusatsu Spa Resort from Volcano Eruption

 25

　Kusatsu Ski and Spa Resort is on the road to recovery after the sudden eruption of Mt. Motoshirane. In January 2017, the volcano erupted on the border of Gunma and Nagano in Japan. Kusatsu is one of the three most famous hot spring resorts in Japan, with a history of spa therapy introduced by a German doctor. The resort receives many snowboarders and skiers. The eruption occurred close to the ski area, and volcanic rocks damaged the chair lifts and gondola system. The town of Kusatsu has announced that it is unlikely to have the gondola reconstructed due to their economic situation. However, using the undamaged facilities and only the bottom part of the slope, Kusatsu will reopen as a resort for beginners and families with kids. As for the spa resort, its reservations were mostly cancelled, resulting in a loss of several hundred million yen in January. However, the town has been sending out messages that the spa is more than five kilometers away from the eruption and that there is no risk. As a result, the number of visitors has recovered to roughly 95% in February (Kusatsu Town, 2018). The town is confident there will be a complete recovery in the near future.

*Reference*
KusatsuTown (2018, March 20). *Heisei Nyukomi Number of 30 February* (The number of guests during February, 2018). Retrieved from http://www.town.kusatsu.gunma.jp/www/contents/1485755746888/index.html

*Notes*
volcano 火山　　eruption 噴火　　erupt 噴火する　　spa therapy 温泉療法

MEMO

# Notetaking

## PRACTICE B

Read Sample Article 2 again. Write notes about the main points here.

|  | Important facts |
|---|---|
| **Where** | Kusatsu Ski and Spa Resort |
| **When** | January 2017 |
| **What happened Why/How** | Volcano eruption |
|  |  |
|  |  |
|  |  |

# Writing a Summary

> **PRACTICE C**
>
> Now that you have read **Sample Article 2** and written notes of the important facts, it is time to write a summary. <u>Without looking at the article again</u>, fill in the blanks in the summary below. Your goal here is to write the same information <u>in your own words</u>.

Visitors are finally coming back to the Kusatsu Ski and Spa Resort after it was

1 _____ a volcano eruption. Although the town 2 _____

_____ the whole ski resort, they were able to reopen by 3 _____

_____ .

In addition, the spa resort had lost a lot of money because 4 _____

_____ . However, the resort has contacted those people to tell them that

5 _____ ,

so 6 _____ .

Thanks to these efforts, the town expects that they will be able to recover from the disaster

soon.

Chapter 12    Summaries

## Practice D

Choose an article from a popular news website and write notes about the main points.

|  | Important facts |
|---|---|
| Where | |
| When | |
| What happened Why/How | |

## Practice E

Now try writing a summary based on the notes you took in **Practice D**. Share your information with your classmates.

# CHAPTER 13   Five Paragraph Essays

In this chapter, we are going to practice writing essays. Essays consist of several paragraphs, so we will carefully look at essay structure. We will first focus on introductory paragraphs.

## Part 1   Introduction

▶ Let's use **Model 1** to learn how to write **the first paragraph** and **the last paragraph**.

1. Quickly read the two paragraphs.
2. Discuss what is mentioned.

---

### Model 1

**The Power of Sports**

**Paragraph 1**

Do you enjoy sports? According to a survey by the Japan Sports Agency (2016), approximately 60% to 70% of the 20,000 respondents had played sports or watched sports games during the past year. Some people had even volunteered at sports events. The survey results also showed that while most people do sports for their health, 37% believe that sports improve communication. Sports are not just hobbies or occupations but have the power to tackle problems in modern society as well.

✳✳✳✳✳✳✳✳✳ Body paragraphs on Page 100 and 101. ✳✳✳✳✳✳✳✳✳

**Paragraph 5**

To conclude, sports can be a powerful tool for solving social problems. Sports can be a means of communication and strengthening bonds among people. Sports also help develop a sense of belonging and may stop population outflow from rural areas. Moreover, sports tourism seems to have a positive economic and cultural impact on local areas. The power of sports is much greater than we imagine and will likely continue to grow as sports marketing and sport tourism expand further.

*Reference*
スポーツ庁 スポーツの実施状況等に関する世論調査（平成 28 年 11 月調査）調査結果の概要 Retrieved from: http://www.mext.go.jp/prev_sports/comp/ b_menu/other/__icsFiles/afieldfile/2017/02/15/1382023_001_1.pdf

*Notes*
Japan Sports Agency 日本スポーツ庁　　ratio 割合　　a sense of belonging 帰属意識
population outflow 人口流出

# Part 2　Structure

Essays consists of at least three paragraphs. We will practice typical five-paragraph essays. The structure is like a burger.

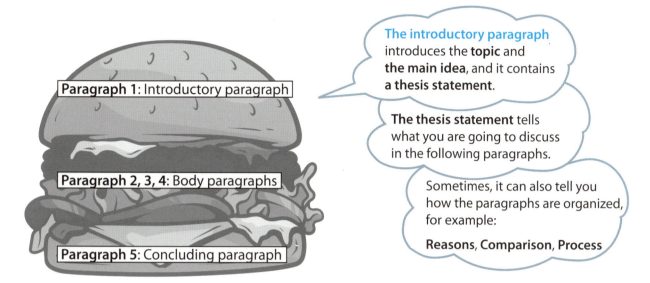

**The introductory paragraph** introduces the **topic** and **the main idea**, and it contains **a thesis statement**.

**The thesis statement** tells what you are going to discuss in the following paragraphs.

Sometimes, it can also tell you how the paragraphs are organized, for example:

**Reasons, Comparison, Process**

▶ Look at **Model 1** again and fill in the blanks.

**Paragraph 1** contains:

**Introduction:** Results of survey by the Japan Sports Agency in 2016

| People | ① do sports |
| | ② 1_____ sports |
| | ③ 2_____ in sports-related events |

| Do sports | ① for 3_____ |
| | ② communication |

**Thesis statement:** _____

**Paragraph 5** starts with a reminder of the thesis statement and ends with a conclusion.

97

▶ Look at the first part of the introductory paragraph in **Model 1**.

> According to a survey by the Japan Sports Agency (2016), approximately 60% of the 20,000 respondents had done some kind of sports during the past year.

This introduction uses **a surprising fact** from a survey to draw the attention of readers.

Ways to introduce a topic include:

| General statements | Interesting stories | Surprising facts | Historical background |

## Introduction strategy

**PRACTICE A**

Discuss which strategy is used. The first one is done for you.

| (fact) | general | history | story |

1. _fact_ — According to a survey by Japan Sports Agency (2016), approximately 60% of the 20,000 respondents had done some kind of sports during the past year.
2. _____ — Unlike several decades before, we can now find almost any products advertised on TV or over the Internet.
3. _____ — In 1992, a container fell off of a cargo ship in the middle of the North Pacific Ocean, and the rubber ducks on board set out on their journey.
4. _____ — We all greet each other more or less, and so do animals.

## Thesis statement

The **thesis statement** is usually **the last sentence of the introductory paragraph**. It includes the essay topic, the writer's idea about the topic, and sometimes a quick list of the supporting points that will be discussed.

> Sports are not just hobbies or occupations but have the power to tackle problems in modern society as well.

This is a strong thesis statement because it includes information about the topic and the focus of the essay.

| The topic | Sports |
|---|---|
| The idea about the topic | Have the power to tackle problems in modern society |
| The supporting points | None |

### PRACTICE B

Look at the thesis statements. Discuss which ones are good thesis statements and which ones are not. Mark ○ for good ones and × for bad ones. 1 is done for you.

1. ○     A sudden increase in the number of tourists can cause problems, such as traffic jams, garbage problems, and accommodation shortages.
2. _____ I will discuss problems caused by tourists in a small town.
3. _____ Student-athletes have to meet the requirements of standard test scores, number of courses in high school, and the grades in those courses.
4. _____ Although most college students work part-time nowadays, a survey has revealed three major problems that students face because of these jobs.
5. _____ Playing college sports is good for your future career.

Sometimes, it is better to avoid using personal language. Instead, refer to evidence.

| Personal language | I think ..., I believe ..., I feel ... |
|---|---|

I think student-athletes are required to manage time well.
➡ Student-athletes are required to manage time well.

I read in an article that working night-shifts negatively affects students' academic performance.
➡ According to an article, working ... (reference)

## Part 3  Writing Tools

## Sub-topics

▶ Let's use **Model 2** and **Model 3** to learn how to organize **body paragraphs**.

**1.** Quickly read the sample article.
**2.** Discuss what it is about.

---

### Model 2

**The Power of Sports**    27

✧✧✧✧✧✧✧✧✧   Introductory paragraph on page 96   ✧✧✧✧✧✧✧✧✧

**Paragraph 2**

( Now / First / The first ), sports may bring people together in places where they no longer gather for community events. The universal rules for sports help with communication among people. This means that even when people have no common language, they can open their hearts, make friends, and share happiness regardless of their ages, nationalities, or abilities. This unique universality of sports can revitalize local communities by offering opportunities for residents to share time.

**Paragraph 3**

( Second, / Another / Also ) power of sports is that they enhance a sense of belonging and may stop population drops in local towns or even whole countries. Sports can help develop stronger connections between people with a common passion. For instance, the Olympic Games and FIFA World Cup™ are two major events that bring people together to cheer for local athletes and teams. The National High School Baseball Tournament in Japan is a similar example. For people who leave their communities because they feel less attached, sports may give a chance to think about their hometown.

✧✧✧✧✧✧✧✧✧   Concluding paragraph on page 96   ✧✧✧✧✧✧✧✧✧

*Notes*
universality 普遍性    feel less attached あまり執着を感じない

## Transitions

**PRACTICE C**

Look at Model 2 again. Circle the appropriate signal to show paragraph transition for Paragraph 2 and Paragraph 3.

---

▶ Look at Model 3 to learn how to **use someone else's information**.

### Model 3

**The Power of Sports**  28

Paragraph 4

Finally, "sport tourism," traveling to engage in or watch sporting activities, increases the number of visitors to event sites. This eventually changes the image and increases the popularity of the area. A successful example is the IRF World Rafting Championship which was held on the Yoshino River in a small city in Tokushima in 2017. Like many other sports, natural features play an important role in rafting. Every year the Great Yoshino River brings 30,000 to 40,000 visitors. According to the *Daily Tokushima*, the city now offers in-service training programs for companies to increase the number of visitors who stay for several days ("Rafting for in-services training, Tour by Mishima City in Tokushima," 2018). Thus, combining nature and sports may assist in the revival of rural areas.

*Reference*
Rafting for in-services, Tour by Mishima City in Tokushima「ラフティングを社員研修に 徳島・三好市、ツアー企画」(2018, January 15). *Daily Tokushima*. Retrieved from http://www.topics.or.jp/localNews/news/2018/01/2018_15159928112666.html

*Notes*
In-service training 社員(社内)研修

## Using somebody else's work or information

▶ Look at Model 3.

> According to the *Daily Tokushima*, the city now offers in-service ...

"According to the *Daily Tokushima*," tells us that the information on in-service training was written in the *Daily Tokushima*.

● **Expressions for referencing**

| According to ..., | **According to** the *Daily Tokushima*, the city now offers in-service training programs for companies. |
|---|---|
| Data shows that ... | **Data shows** an increase in the number of tourists to Tokushima. |
| The graph indicates that ... | **The graph indicates that** tourists stay more than two days in the city. |
| The investigation demonstrates that ... | **The investigation** clearly **demonstrates** positive effects of the rafting event on tourism. |
| The editor states/claims/reports/argues that ... | **The editor states/clams/reports/argues that** many other local cities can also hold such events. |

## Some rules for in-text citation and references

When you use sources for your writing, insert an **in-text citation** directly after the words or ideas you have used from those sources. At the end of your writing, you will list all the sources you referred to. This is done so that the readers are able to go to the source for details.

| | | |
|---|---|---|
| **Example 1**<br><br>**News article** | In-text citation | According to the *Daily Tokushima*, the city now offers in-service training programs for companies to increase the number of visitors who stay for several days. ("Rafting for in-service training, Tour by Mishima City in Tokushima," 2018). |
| | General format | (Author, Year) For articles with no author, (Title, Year). |
| | Reference | Rafting for in-service training, Tour by Mishima City in Tokushima (2018, January 15). *Tokushima Shimbun*. Retrieved from: http://www.topics.or.jp/localNews/news/2018/01/2018_15159928112666.html |
| | General format | Author, A. (Year, Month Day). Title of article. Title of Magazine/Newspapers in Italics. Retrieved from http://URL |

| | | |
|---|---|---|
| **Example 2**<br><br>**Report** | In-text citation | According to a survey by Japan Sports Agency (2016), ~~~~.<br>*When the author is mentioned in the sentence, only the year is shown. |
| | General format | ... Author (Year) .... |
| | Reference | Japan Sports Agency (2017). Summary of an opinion survey on sports (November 2016). Retrieved from http://www.mext.go.jp/prev_sports/comp/b_menu/other/__icsFiles/afieldfile/2017/02/15/1382023_001_1.pdf |
| | General format | Author, A. (Year). Title of report. Retrieved from http://URL |

● **Major styles of citation**

APA Style: American Psychology Association
MLA Style: Modern Language Association
Chicago Style: Chicago

## Part 4　Writing

## Outlining

When thinking about what to write, outlining is one way to organize ideas.

> **PRACTICE D**
>
> Write an outline in a pair or group on the following topic.
> 1. Choose the kind of introduction you are going to use, and write your ideas.
> 2. Write an outline and the thesis statement.

| Topic | Greetings in different cultures | | |
|---|---|---|---|
| Introductory Paragraph | Introduction | General idea | |
| | | Story | |
| | | Fact | |
| | | Background | |
| | Thesis statement | | |
| Body Paragraph 1 | | | |
| Body Paragraph 2 | | | |
| Body Paragraph 3 | | | |
| Concluding Paragraph | | | |

# CHAPTER 14   Concluding Paragraphs for Essays

We are going to practice writing concluding paragraphs for essays. We will also look at how to organize body paragraphs.

## Part 1   Introduction

▶ Let's use **Model 1** to learn how to write **the last** paragraph for an academic essay.

1. Quickly read the two paragraphs.
2. Discuss what is mentioned.

### Model 1

**Cultural Differences and Coaching Styles**  29

**Paragraph 1**

It is often the case that coaches and athletes on a team do not have the same cultural background. In the Japan Professional Football League's top league, J1, 6 out of 18 teams are led by foreign head coaches (J.LEAGUE, 2018). There are also a number of foreign players in the league. In such cases, the coaching styles may be different from coaching in a mono-cultural environment. A group of researchers conducted an interview survey on elite or top-class gymnastics coaches in the United States. They investigated coaches' perceptions of cross-cultural matters. The survey results revealed the differences and similarities in cultural awareness and coaching styles.

✻✻✻✻✻✻✻✻✻✻✻✻ Body paragraphs on page 107 ✻✻✻✻✻✻✻✻✻✻✻✻

**Paragraph 5**

To sum up, coaches who were involved in this survey showed differences and similarities in how they think about the cultural gaps between themselves and the athletes they coach. Decisions on whether to modify their coaching according to the athletes' cultural backgrounds were also different. However, the coaches agreed that it is difficult to deal with cultural differences and that clear team rules and mutual respect are essential for successful coaching. As borders continue to disappear in the world of sports, more coaches and athletes will be active in cross-cultural environments. In such cases, the coach's cultural competence and respect for athletes' varying cultures will be essential.

*References*

Sasaba, I., Fitzpatrick, S.J., Pope-Rhodius, A., & Sakuma, H. (2017). Elite gymnastics coaches' perceptions of coaching athletes from different cultures. *International Journal of Coaching Science, 11*(1), 15-30.
J.LEAGUE (2018). Retrieved on March 31, 2018. https://data.j-league.or.jp/

*Notes*

**elite athletes** プロ選手やオリンピック選手などのトップ選手     **gymnastics** 体操競技     **perception** 受けとめ方
**awareness** 気づき

## Part 2  Structure

### Concluding paragraph

Introductory paragraph → Body paragraphs → Concluding paragraph

**The concluding paragraph** reminds readers what was discussed. It usually ends with **suggestions**, **predictions**, or **judgments**.

▶ Fill in the information below for **Model 1**. (two instances)

| Thesis statement |  |
|---|---|
| Paragraph 5 starts with |  |
| Paragraph 5 ends with |  |

▶ Fill in the information below for **Model 1** "The Power of Sports" in Chapter 13 on page 96.

| Thesis statement |  |
|---|---|
| Paragraph 5 starts with |  |
| Paragraph 5 ends with |  |

▶ Look at how the essay is concluded. There are some different endings.

① Judgments / Most important point
② Predictions
③ Suggestions

▶ Discuss what kind of closing strategy is used for the endings above.

1. Ending of "Cultural Differences and Coaching Styles"  ( **Model 1** in Chapter 14 )  _____
2. Ending of "The Power of Sports"  ( **Model 1** in Chapter 13 )  _____

## Restating the thesis in concluding paragraphs

> **PRACTICE A**
>
> Look at the thesis statements below and paraphrase them so that they can be used in concluding paragraphs.

1. Coaches and athletes are sometimes frustrated because of cultural conflicts between them.

2. My favorite city in the US was Boston because of the friendly people who made me feel welcome and the wide variety of stores and restaurants available.

3. After working as a teacher for a couple of years, I decided to go to graduate school to further develop my teaching skills and start my career as a researcher.

● **Concluding paragraph checklist**

| | |
|---|---|
| Have I restated my thesis statement? | Yes / No |
| Have I summarized the body paragraphs in the same order? | Yes / No |
| Have I used the keywords? | Yes / No |
| Have I ended the paragraph with a relevant suggestion, prediction, or judgment? | Yes / No |

## Model 1 (Continued)

### Cultural Differences and Coaching Styles

✳✳✳✳✳✳✳✳ Introductory paragraph on page 104 ✳✳✳✳✳✳✳✳

**Paragraph 2**

The first difference among the coaches is their awareness level of the cultural differences between themselves and their athletes. Some elite coaches do observe the differences among their athletes. However, most of them take the differences as individual differences rather than cultural differences. To identify cultural differences could even be regarded as cultural discrimination. Other coaches, although aware of the cultural differences, choose to avoid discussion on this topic. This way, they can focus on unifying the team rather than pointing out differences.

**Paragraph 3**

Second, the stance taken by individual coaches also varies greatly. Some coaches, although fully being aware of the cultural differences, do not change their coaching style at all. This is because those coaches do not believe it is necessary to adapt their styles to diverse cultures. To them, cultural differences do not matter in universal team sports. On the other hand, some coaches adapt their coaching style after observing and learning about these differences. In some cases, a coach may tailor how he or she communicates with athletes from different cultural backgrounds. For example, Americans and Middle Easterners like to criticize directly and often use sarcasm, while Japanese players do not. There are other coaches who are somewhat in between the opposing sides. Though they do not change their program nor their approach, they try to be understanding.

**Paragraph 4**

Although the awareness and stance of coaches toward cross-cultural issues may differ, there are also some similarities. For one thing, most coaches have had difficulties dealing with athletes of different cultures. A Western-oriented coach expressed discomfort in the way young athletes were punished in China and Japan because he believed results would not come with violent coaching. Second, some coaches commonly mention that the key to successful coaching is to establish team rules and to respect each other. Making and understanding team rules is essential, as is having a consensus on what will happen when the rules are violated. In addition, in any culture, by showing respect and treating everyone equally, coaches can earn their athletes' trust.

✳✳✳✳✳✳✳✳ Concluding paragraph on page 104 ✳✳✳✳✳✳✳✳

## Part 3  Writing Tools

▶ Look at the three body paragraphs in **Model 1** on page 107. How does each paragraph begin?

Paragraph 2 (Body 1) starts with _____

Paragraph 3 (Body 2) starts with _____

Paragraph 4 (Body 3) starts with _____

Each body paragraph should be relevant to the thesis statement. They should also follow a clear logical order.

▶ Let's use **Model 2** to look at the **essay organization**. The paragraphs are shuffled.

**1.** Put the paragraphs in the correct order.

**2.** Add a signal to each paragraph.

| In summary | Another | The first | Finally |

① If you have ever visited another country, …

② _____ difference is how both cultures solve social problems.

③ _____, the two cultures have very different views on various aspects of society.

④ _____, attitudes regarding work are different in both countries, as well.

⑤ _____ difference is their attitudes regarding individualism.

## Model 2

**Japan and the U.S.A.: Social Differences**  31

① If you have ever visited another country, there is a good chance you were that foreigner who did something strange. Cultural and social differences between countries can sometimes be quite large, making the behavior of people from other countries seem strange. Japan and the United States are good examples of this issue. Japanese people and Americans do not always share the same values, which causes differences in how they approach certain social situations.

108

② _____ difference is how both cultures solve social problems. Japanese people like to avoid face-to-face arguments whenever possible, so if they have a problem with something, they will often choose to complain indirectly. For example, if an apartment neighbor is being noisy, Japanese people will usually contact the landlord. In doing so, they can avoid embarrassing their neighbor. Americans would actually be insulted by this behavior. In the same situation, they would most likely speak to their neighbors about the problem directly. In their minds, involving more people only makes the problem bigger and causes unnecessary embarrassment. Therefore, despite having the same motivation, Japanese people and Americans would solve the problem very differently.

③ _____, the two cultures have very different views on various aspects of society. Japanese people favor a group mentality, dislike confrontation, and value formality. Americans promote individualism, confront people directly, and avoid formality as much as possible. These opposing views naturally create different opinions about what is normal in both countries. Therefore, visitors and foreign residents in both countries should remain aware in order to avoid embarrassing or awkward situations.

④ _____, attitudes regarding work are different in both countries, as well. In Japan, the process is just as important as the result. Accuracy and organization are top priorities. Japan is known to require extensive paperwork for everything. As a result, many application processes take time, but mistakes are kept to a minimum. In the U.S., reaching the goal quickly is the most important thing. Americans are more willing to bend rules, take shortcuts, or skip steps if they can accomplish their tasks in less time. Formalities are often considered to be a burden. Therefore, Americans get impatient with Japanese procedures, while Japanese people consider Americans to be careless.

⑤ _____ difference is their attitudes regarding individualism. In general, Japanese people favor a group mentality and try to blend in as much as possible. There is a saying in Japan: "The nail that sticks out gets hammered down." An example of this is clearly visible when Japanese university students are job hunting; every job applicant is expected to have the same black suit and hair color, and most never try to be different. On the other hand, Americans focus more on people as individuals and do their best to stand out. When applying for jobs, many people choose to wear bright shirts and neckties in order to be more memorable. In almost any field, creativity and outside-the-box ideas are usually appreciated. Differences like these affect the way Japanese people and Americans view individuals in society.

*Notes*
individualism 個人主義　group mentality 集団志向　get hammered 打たれる　applicant 応募者
landlord 家主（大家）　be insulted by … …に侮辱される　top priorities 最優先事項
extensive paperwork 膨大な書類事務　formalities 形式的なこと　confrontation 対立　confront 対立する
outside-the-box-ideas 枠にとらわれない考え

## PRACTICE B

Complete the outline for Model 2.

| Introductory paragraph | Introduction | |
|---|---|---|
| | Thesis statement | |
| Body paragraphs | 1 First sentence | |
| | 2 First sentence | |
| | 3 First sentence | |
| Concluding paragraph | | |

● **Expressions for discussion**

When writing an essay based on some information or evidence, use expressions such as:

| Future prediction | Auxiliary | will>may>{might, would} | Smartphone and tablet markets **will** continue to expand in the next decade. |
|---|---|---|---|
| | Adverbs | probably, perhaps, possibly | The sales of electronic dictionaries **may** decrease if more people begin using dictionary apps on tablets. |
| Possibility | Auxiliary | can>could | In Japan, however, student users **can** support the electronic dictionary business. |
| Avoiding definitive statements | Frequency adverbs | not always, often, sometimes, usually | Although dictionary apps **seem** convenient for the smartphone generation, buying one electronic dictionary is **sometimes** less expensive than using several dictionary apps. |
| | Verbs | seem, tend to | School teachers **tend to** recommend dictionaries over dictionary apps. |

## PRACTICE C

Look at Model 2 again. Circle the expressions listed in the box above. Discuss why the expressions are used.

Chapter 14   Concluding Paragraphs for Essays

## Part 4   Writing

### PRACTICE D

Work alone, with your parter, or in a group. Choose one topic from the following list. Write an outline for a comparison/contrast essay.

① hybrid cars and electric cars   ② direct vs. indirect lighting
③ how people take vacation   ④ personal space
⑤ different housing   ⑥ different food   ⑦ celebrations

| Introductory paragraph | |
|---|---|
| Body paragraphs | 1 |
| | 2 |
| | 3 |
| Concluding paragraph | |

## Writing process

### PRACTICE E

Based on the outline above, write a thesis statement. Next, write a draft of one body paragraph.

| Thesis statement | |
|---|---|
| Draft of one body paragraph | |

111

# CHAPTER 15  Effective Ways to Begin an Essay

We are going to practice **effective ways to begin an essay**. We will also look at **how to find ways to improve our own writing**.

## Part 1    Introduction

▶ Let's use **Model 1** to learn how to write **longer introductory paragraphs**.

1. Quickly read the essay.
2. Discuss what is mentioned.

### Model 1

**Mindfulness, Why Not?**  32

Every Thursday afternoon, during lunchtime, about a hundred people gather at the UCLA Hammer Museum Theatre in Los Angeles. Teenagers, office workers, and elderly people simply come in and sit down quietly. They practice "mindfulness meditation" guided by Ms. Diana Winston, the Director of Education at the UCLA Mindful Awareness Research Center (Weekly Podcast at the Hammer, 2017). It is free and always open to the general public. In western countries, mindfulness is growing in popularity and the benefits are being recognized in various fields.

Mindfulness is defined as "Awareness that arises through paying attention, on purpose, in the present moment, non-judgmentally (Kabat-Zinn, 2003)." "Mindfulness" is the English translation of "Sati" in Pali, which means "awareness" or "recollection." As you can imagine, current mindfulness practices come from ancient Buddhism, but are now used unrelated to the religion. Although sitting meditation is well known as a formal practice, a variety of methods including yoga and certain body movements can also deepen mindfulness.

Mindfulness practices have three major effects. First, they help us stay in control of our thinking. For example, our minds are often in so-called "autopilot mode" while we are texting or browsing over the internet. That is, our minds are automatically thinking, wondering, or planning something. Our minds can stay fully in the present by practicing mindfulness. We can also distance ourselves from thoughts such as regrets and worries. This distance leads to deeper awareness in daily life and even stress reduction. Moreover, a growing number of neuroscience studies now reveal that continuous mindfulness practice changes our brain structure (Tang et al., 2015). Those changes may improve the ability to memorize, control our impulses, and create positive emotions. Indeed, mindfulness is an evidence-based practice that can enrich our lives.

Because the positive effects of mindfulness meditation have been proven, more than 6,000 schools across America currently offer classes for it as part of the regular curriculum. A variety of mindfulness-based clinical methods are now bringing about a "revolution" in social work, clinical psychology, and psychiatry settings. Professionals use these new methods to treat various problems, including eating disorders, substance abuse, and post-traumatic symptoms. Using meditation as treatment gives us alternatives to medications that may have harmful side effects.

The National Institute of Health shows that more than 18 million people routinely practice mindfulness meditation in America (Clarke et al., 2015). Now that we know about mindfulness and its positive effects, the gates of its benefits are wide open to us. No expensive gadgets are required. Why not knock on the door of mindfulness today?

*References*
Clarke, T. C., Black L. I., Stussman, B. J., Barnes, P. M., & Nahin, R. L. (2015). Trends in the use of complementary health approaches among adults: United States, 2002–2012. *National health statistics reports; no 79.* Hyattsville, MD: National Center for Health Statistics.
Kabat-Zinn, J. (2003). Mindfulness-based stress reduction (MBSR). *Constructivism in the Human Sciences*, 8(2), 73-107.
Tang, Y. Y., Holzel, B. K., & Posner, M. I. (2015). The neuroscience of mindfulness meditation. *Nature Reviews Neuroscience, 16*(4), 213-225.
Weekly Podcast at the Hammer (2017). Retrieved from http://marc.ucla.edu/meditation-at-the-hammer

*Notes*
Pali パリ語、中期インド - アリアン語でサンスクリット語に似た言語　　auto-pilot 自動操縦　　distance 距離をおく
neuroscience 神経科学　　impulse 衝動　　clinical psychology 臨床心理　　psychiatry 精神医学
eating disorders 摂食障害　　substance abuse 薬物乱用　　post-traumatic symptoms PTSD
alternative to ... …の代わり

## Part 2　Structure

▶ Write the first sentence of the introductory paragraph.

---

▶ What kind of information is given after the first sentence?
　　a) opinions　　b) historical information　　c) statistics　　d) current situation

▶ Write the thesis statement.

## Hooks

The first sentence of the introductory paragraph is called the "hook". The purpose of the hook is to catch the reader's attention. It should make the reader interested in reading the rest of the essay.

### ● Hook types

There are different types of **hooks** you can use.

1) A question
2) A quote
3) An interesting statement
4) A surprising statistic
5) A common truth

▶▶ **Model 1** uses **an interesting statement**.

"A hundred people standing outside of the UCLA Hammer Museum Theatre" is not normal, so the reader will naturally wonder, "Why?"

## Building sentences

The sentences that give information after the hook and before the thesis statement are called **building sentences**. These sentences help introduce the topic by giving background information before the main argument is introduced.

### ● Building sentence types

There are different kinds of **building sentences** you can use.

1) Explaining the current situation
2) Giving statistics about the topic
3) Telling the history of the topic
4) Expressing common opinions about the topic

▶▶ **Model 1** explains **the current situation** by giving a current example of mindful meditation being practiced at UCLA.

## Practice A

Here are 5 hooks that could be used for **Model 1**. Write the hook type for each.

① A question  ② A quote  ③ An interesting statement
④ A surprising statistic  ⑤ A common truth

| | Hook type | |
|---|---|---|
| 1. | | According to a recent survey, more adults and children are practicing mindfulness meditation. |
| 2. | | Have you heard of mindfulness? |
| 3. | | Everyone could benefit from a little extra concentration. |
| 4. | | A hundred people gathered outside the UCLA Hammer Museum Theatre. |
| 5. | | "The best way to capture moments is to pay attention. This is how we cultivate mindfulness. Mindfulness means being awake. It means knowing what you are doing."<br>~Jon Kabat-Zinn |

## Practice B

Choose the correct building sentence type for these introductory sentences in an essay about "the causes of university student fatigue."

Current situation   Statistics   History   Common opinions

| | Building sentence type | Introductory sentences |
|---|---|---|
| 1. | | In universities across the country, you can see students who are too tired to keep their eyes open in class. Even worse, some students do not have the energy to get out of bed in the morning. |
| 2. | | In 2013, the American College Health Association reported that about 46% of university students felt overwhelmed with the amount of assignments and tests in their classes. Many students also said that their high stress levels also affected their ability to study or complete their homework. |

(http://www.acha-ncha.org/docs/ACHA-NCHA-II_UNDERGRAD_ReferenceGroup_ExecutiveSummary_Spring2013.pdf)

## Part 3 — Writing Tools

### Revising essays

Avoiding repetitive or overly used words

● **Avoid redundancy**

Be careful not to use words that have the same meaning together.

Ex  Ask your partner to fix ~~and correct~~ your mistakes.
It is better not to repeat the same word ~~again and again~~.

● **Avoid using the same words too often**

Use words that have the same meaning in different sentences.

Ex  Ask your partner to <u>fix</u> your mistakes. Submit your essay after you <u>correct</u> all of the mistakes together.

● **Use pronouns**

When you have to mention the same subject or object many times, pronouns help your writing sound better.

Ex  <u>The car</u> will not start. <u>The car</u> is out of gas.  ➡  <u>The car</u> will not start. <u>It</u> is out of gas.

▶▶ Let's use **Model 2** to review how essays are structured.

1. Paragraphs A, B, C, and D are shuffled. Discuss the correct order in a pair or a group.

2. Underline repetitive or overly used words and discuss how you can revise them.

### Model 2

**Language Support for Non-Japanese Speaking Children**  33

   A  In addition to supporting Japanese language development, heritage language support is also important. Many people agree that the development of the mother language, or family language, is very essential for intellectual development, emotional stability, and identity formation. The Canadian government has long been making an effort to tackle and solve this issue. On the other hand, the Japanese education system focuses on Japanese language instruction while often neglecting heritage language teaching.

**B**  In Japan, the number of schoolchildren who need Japanese language support reached 40,000 in 2015 (MEXT, 2017), and the number of those schoolchildren is increasing. These children came from various countries or were born to foreign parents in Japan, and these children have acquired oral languages other than Japanese. It is no doubt that those children need special support in learning Japanese, but they also need support in maintaining and developing their heritage languages.

**C**  While supporting heritage language learners with their Japanese schoolwork is now quite common, systematic and effective heritage language support needs to be established as well. As the foreign population in Japan continues to increase more and more, there will be a larger demand for supporting non-Japanese residents. This young multilingual population will become a valuable resource for Japan in the future.

**D**  As for the Japanese language, some local schools and communities have been supporting schoolchildren with their schoolwork. For example, volunteers gather and help children after school, on weekends, and during summer vacation. A study has shown that although it is rather easy to acquire basic communication skills, it is often difficult to master the academic language necessary to achieve successful school grades. This is often due to insufficient reading skills. Unlike oral language proficiency, literacy skill acquisition requires time and effort.

*Reference*
MEXT Retrieved from http:// www.mext.go.jp/b_menu/houdou/29/06 /__icsFiles/ afieldfile/2017/06/21/1386753.pdf

*Notes*
**heritage language** 継承言語（継承言語とは、移住者が親から受け継ぐ言語で、社会で使われている言語とは異なる。）
**neglecting** 無視して    **intellectual development** 知的発達    **emotional stability** 情緒的安定性
**identity formation** アイデンティティの形成    **oral language** 口頭言語・話ことば    **residents** 住人
**acquisition** 獲得    **literacy skills** 読み書き技能

## PRACTICE C

Complete the sentences by writing words that have similar meanings to the underlined words. Choose from the words in the box.

| wonderful | simple | comfortable | it | powerful |
| he | new | gorgeous | normal | hard |

1. My brother does not like heavy metal. _____ prefers dance music.
2. This is an easy test. The questions are really _____.
3. The United States is a strong country with a _____ army.
4. You wrote a great story. You gave _____ descriptions of the scenery, so I felt like I was actually there.
5. You have to try on this dress! It's beautiful. You are going to look so _____ in it.

# Part 4 Writing

> **PRACTICE D**
> Brainstorm additional topics with your partner or group. Then, write the hook and building sentences for your introductory paragraph. Finally, write the main ideas for your body paragraphs.

## Topic examples

- Enjoy university life
- Are theme parks only for children?
- _____

- Problems with bicycles
- _____
- _____

| Topic | | |
|---|---|---|
| **Introductory paragraph** | Hook | |
| | Building sentence | |
| | Thesis statement | |
| **Body paragraphs** | 1 | |
| | 2 | |
| | 3 | |
| **Concluding paragraph** | Summary of main points / Paraphrased thesis statement | |

## Practice E

Write an essay based on your outline.

▶ Before you submit your essay, make sure to double check it.

|  |  | Self | Peer |
|---|---|---|---|
| **Mechanics** | Punctuation marks and capital letters are correctly used. |  |  |
|  | Spelling is checked. |  |  |
| **Format** | The essay is formatted as the instructor specified. |  |  |
|  | In case of digital submission, the file name is detailed as specified. |  |  |
| **Structure** | The essay has an introductory paragraph, body paragraphs, and a concluding paragraph. |  |  |
| **Introductory Paragraph** | There is a hook, building sentences, and a clear thesis statement. |  |  |
| **Body** | Each body paragraph discusses the main idea. |  |  |
|  | The body paragraphs are presented in a clear order. |  |  |
| **Concluding Paragraph** | The main points are summarized or the thesis statement is restated. |  |  |
| **Plagiarism** | Outside information was paraphrased and the sources were cited. |  |  |
| **References** | Reference list includes all the works used (cited) in my essay in an appropriate format. |  |  |

## Peer review

**PRACTICE F**

Read an essay written by your classmates. Check it using the checklist on page 120. Write comments and questions.

Comment

Questions

# APPENDICES  Writing Tools

● **Capitalization** (Chapter 1, p. 9)

| Sentence beginning | There are…. Local sports…. |
|---|---|
| Names of places, people, and groups | Tokyo, California, Hokkaido |
| | Miyazaki Hayao |
| | Japan Sports Association |
| **Title:** Capitalize the initial letters of every word in a title except prepositions and articles. When a title starts with an article, the first letter of the article is capitalized. | The Benefit of After-school Sports Clubs in Japan |
| | The Roles of Local Sports Associations |
| | Around the World |

● **Comma rules** (Chapter 2, p. 16)

| After signals | First, Second, Finally, |
|---|---|
| Before "and," "but," "so" | Commas did not exist in classic Japanese, but they are used in modern Japanese. |
| because …, when …, if …, although … | Although Japanese is written both horizontally and vertically, the same Japanese commas are used.<br>When western literature was brought to Japan, commas were introduced into the Japanese writing system.<br>It is said that if emperor of the Meiji Era had not loved Western novels, there would not have been commas in Japanese writing. |
| Listing | Unlike Japanese, English commas are used before "and," "but," and "so." |

● **Comma rules** (Chapter 11, p. 85)

| Commas after signals | Commas after subordinate clauses |
|---|---|
| **To begin,** remember that you should enjoy reading. | **If** you are going to be late for dinner, you should text somebody in the family. |
| **First,** try a book of an easy level series and read some more from the same series. | **As soon as** everybody comes home, they start cooking. |
| **Second/Next,** when you can read quite fluently, move on to the next level. | **When** everybody is seated, the dinner starts with a prayer. |
| **Then,** stay at the same level until you become comfortable at the level. | **Until** everybody finishes, you are not supposed to leave the table. |
| | **Before** you leave the table, remember to thank the cooks for the dinner. |

● **Signals for supporting sentences** (Chapter 2, p. 13)

| Signals | First, Second, Third, Next, Finally, In addition, Moreover |
|---|---|

● **Signals for concluding sentences** (Chapter 3, p. 19)

| Signals | In summary, In conclusion, To conclude, Therefore, Overall, All in all,···. |
|---|---|

● **Signals for opinions and reasons** (Chapter 3, p. 22)

| Phrases to introduce opinions | Words to connect ideas to reasons |
|---|---|
| In my opinion, P.E. is necessary for three reasons. | because (use before the reason)<br>　I am happy because today is a holiday.<br>× 　Today is a holiday because I am happy. |
| I believe/think that regular exercise helps children develop their physical ability. | so (use after the reason)<br>　Today is a holiday, so I am happy. |

● **Signals for details and examples** (Chapter 4, p. 25)

| To give details | Furthermore, In addition, Additionally, Moreover, In other words, Also |
|---|---|
| To give examples | For example, For instance, Another example is … |

● **Signals for comparing** (Chapter 5, p. 33)

| | | |
|---|---|---|
| Comparing words | like | Like soccer, basketball is a sport that requires a lot of physical stamina. |
| | similar to | American football is similar to soccer in that it is also a team sport of eleven players. |
| | both | A balanced diet and regular exercise are both necessary to keep our bodies strong and healthy. |
| | neither | Neither Sakina nor her mother knew how to change the tire, so they asked their neighbor for help. |
| Comparing sentences | similarly | If you are trying to lose weight, running is a good way to burn calories. Similarly, swimming is a great exercise that allows you to move your whole body. |

## ● Signals for contrasting (Chapter 6, p. 41)

| | | |
|---|---|---|
| **Contrasting words and phrases** | B **is different from** A. | British English is **different from** American English in several ways. |
| | A **and** B **differ**. | American English **and** British English **differ**. |
| | **Unlike** A, B …. | **Unlike** British English, American English spells words more as they sound. |
| **Contrasting sentences/ clauses** | A …, **but** B …. | You normally walk into a building on the first floor in America, **but** this same floor is called "ground floor" in Britain. |
| | A …. **However,** B …. | A popular means of transportation is the "subway" in America. **However,** it is called the "underground" or "tube" in Britain. |
| | A …. **On the other hand** / **In contrast** / **Conversely** / **However,** B …. | This laptop company offers a five-year guarantee. **On the other hand** / **In contrast** / **Conversely** / **However**, that laptop is covered only for one year. |
| | **While** A …, B …. | **While** laptop A is fast with a large screen, laptop B is small and light in weight. |

## ● Signals for cause and effect (Chapter 7, p. 49)

| | Signal words | |
|---|---|---|
| **Adverb/ Adverbial phrases** | therefore/thus/ consequently | The student seldom came to class and missed many of the assignments. **Therefore**, it was no surprise that he failed the course. |
| | for this reason | The roads in mountain towns become icy and slippery during the cold winter season. **For this reason**, many larger vehicles can be seen with chains covering their tires. |
| | as a result | The number of children in each of the schools continued to decrease. **As a result**, the schools had no choice but to close two of the campuses and combine their students. |
| **Clauses** | because/since | **Since** it is raining, I have decided not to go jogging today. |
| **Phrases** | because of | Many university graduates say that the first two years in their companies are the toughest **because of** the long hours they have to work. |
| | due to | **Due to** the strong winds and heavy rains caused by the typhoon, all of the fireworks festivals were cancelled last weekend. |

## ● Signals for evidence (Chapter 8, p. 57)

| For & against | Proponents/Opponents argue that … |
|---|---|
| | Supporters / People who [are for/against, agree/disagree] |
| Contrasting sentences/clauses | while, although |
| | On the other hand, In contrast, Conversely, However |
| Referencing | According to …, Some people [argue, claim, state, believe] that … |
| | It has been found/reported that …, Studies have found that …, Research shows that …, Data shows … |

## ● Descriptive word order (Chapter 4, p. 27)

| | opinion | size→age→shape→color | origin | material |
|---|---|---|---|---|
| a, an, the, these, those, two, 11, 1500 | sweet, sour, salty, spicy, mild, pungent, pleasant, soft, rough | large, long, short, round, square | European, Asian, Japanese | woolen, cotton, wood |

## ● Rules for comparing/contrasting using adjectives and adverbs (Chapter 5, p. 36)

| | |
|---|---|
| and … too<br><br>and so … | Mariko is allergic to pollen, and Miyuki is allergic to pollen.<br>→ Mariko is allergic to pollen, **and Miyuki is, too**.<br>→ Mariko is allergic to pollen, **and so is Miyuki**.<br><br>American football involves physical contact, and rugby involves physical contact.<br>→ American football involves body contact, **and rugby does, too**.<br>→ American football involves body contact, **and so does rugby**. |
| and … either<br><br>and neither … | Airplane tickets to Hawaii are not cheap, and tickets to Australia are not cheap, either.<br>→ Airplane tickets to Hawaii are not cheap, **and tickets to Australia are not either**.<br>→ Airplane tickets to Hawaii are not cheap, and **neither are tickets to Australia**.<br><br>Mariko has not been to TDL, and some of her friends have not been to TDL, either.<br>→ Mariko has not been to TDL, **and some of her friends have not either**.<br>→ Mariko has not been to TDL, **and neither have some of her friends**. |

● **Auxiliary verbs** (Chapter 9, p. 65)

|  | Auxiliary verbs | Examples |
|---|---|---|
| For possibility | can | Unhealthy eating habits **can** lead to health problems as you get older. |
| | could | You **could** suffer from diabetes. |
| For future and hypothetical situations | will | Adding ramps to each entrance **will** make the building barrier-free. |
| | may | People in wheelchairs **may** choose to visit the restaurant. |
| | would | If someone posted that the restaurant has barrier-free facilities, more people **would** plan to visit the restaurant. |

● **Gerund** (Chapter 9, p. 68)

| Verb | Gerund | Example |
|---|---|---|
| put | putting | **Putting** quotation marks at the beginning and end of your quoted sentence shows that you are borrowing the idea. |
| tell | telling | **Telling** the reader where you found the information is necessary for this too. |
| avoid | avoiding | The most important step in **avoiding** plagiarism is doing your own work. |
| copy | copying | **Copying** someone else's writing will get you into trouble. |

● **Expressions for discussion** (Chapter 14, p. 110)

| Future prediction | Auxiliary | will>may> {might, would} | Smartphone and tablet markets **will** continue to expand in the next decade. |
|---|---|---|---|
| | Adverbs | probably, perhaps, possibly | The sales of electronic dictionaries **may** decrease if more people begin using dictionary apps on tablets. |
| Possibility | Auxiliary | can>could | In Japan, however, student users **can** support the electronic dictionary business. |
| Avoiding definitive statements | Frequency adverbs | not always, often, sometimes, usually | Although dictionary apps **seem** convenient for the smartphone generation, buying one electronic dictionary is **sometimes** less expensive than using several dictionary apps. |
| | Verbs | seem, tend to | School teachers **tend to** recommend dictionaries over dictionary apps. |

著作権法上、無断複写・複製は禁じられています。

---

## Real Writing　　　　　　　　　　　　　　　　　　　　　　[B-886]
From structured paragraph to complete essay
大学生のためのエッセイライティング入門

| | | |
|---|---|---|
| 1　刷 | 2019年 4月 1日 | |
| 7　刷 | 2024年 9月 1日 | |
| 著　者 | 川﨑　眞理子 | Mariko Kawasaki |
| | アイエド・ハセイン | Ayed Hasian |
| | サミュエル・ホー | Samuel Haugh |
| | 中野　陽子 | Yoko Nakano |
| | 茨木　正志郎 | Seishirou Ibaraki |
| 発行者 | 南雲　一範　　Kazunori Nagumo | |
| 発行所 | 株式会社　南雲堂 | |
| | 〒162-0801　東京都新宿区山吹町361 | |
| | NAN'UN-DO Co., Ltd. | |
| | 361 Yamabuki-cho, Shinjuku-ku, Tokyo 162-0801, Japan | |
| | 振替口座：00160-0-46863 | |
| | TEL: 03-3268-2311（営業部：学校関係） | |
| | 　　　 03-3268-2384（営業部：書店関係） | |
| | 　　　 03-3268-2387（編集部） | |
| | FAX: 03-3269-2486 | |
| 編　集 | 加藤　敦 | |
| 製　版 | 木内　早苗 | |
| 装　丁 | 銀月堂 | |
| 検　印 | 省　略 | |
| コード | ISBN978-4-523-17886-6　C0082 | |

Printed in Japan

E-mail　nanundo@post.email.ne.jp
URL　https://www.nanun-do.co.jp/